REALty Feng Shui:
Places and Profits in the Marketplace

Johndennis and Anita Govert

REALty Feng Shui: Places and Profits in the Marketplace

Copyright © 2018 by Johndennis and Anita Govert
Zengo House
Tucson, Arizona
www.realtyfengshui.net
www.zengohouse.com
2017

Other Books by Johndennis Govert
And the Lake is Full of Water
Feng Shui: Art and Harmony of Place

Published by

Zengo House

Tucson, Arizona, USA

All rights reserved. © Johndennis and Anita Govert 2017. All text is by Johndennis and Anita Govert. All images and shodo are by Johndennis Govert unless where otherwise noted.

No part of this book may be reproduced or transmitted in any form or by any means, electronic or mechanical, including photocopying, recording or by any information storage and retrieval system, without written permission from the authors, except in the case of brief quotations embodied in critical articles or reviews.

Layout design by Andrea Brooks
First Edition: 2018
ISBN: 978-0-9995731-1-2

For all the Worlds' Saints, Sages and Bodhisattvas
For Our Revered Gurus and Students
For All Who Seek to Benefit Others

Table of Contents

INTRODUCTION .... **ix**
    Place, the Final Frontier xiv

CHAPTER 1: HOW FENG SHUI WORKS **1**

CHAPTER 2: WEBS OF RELATIONSHIPS **11**
    Feng Shui as Webs of Relationships 13
    Client Relationships 15
    The Generic Relationship 19
    Advice for Sellers and Their Agents 21
    "Ode on a Bungalow" Advice for Buyers and Their Agents 23
    Advice to Agents with Asian Clients 25
    Advice to Asian Agents with Non-Asian Clients 26
    Advice for Heirs and Estate Agents from Beyond the Pale 28

CHAPTER 3: FENG SHUI WORLD VIEWS **31**
    Systems of Feng Shui 33
    It's All Relative 37

CHAPTER 4: LEARN FROM HISTORY **39**
    The Best Market Research 50
    Mixed Life and Business Patterns 51

CHAPTER 5: ACCELERATING THE WHOLE SALE **53**
    Rituals That Create Wanted Change 54
    Emptying as Dissolution 55
    Creation Rituals 58
    Clearing the Air 58

Centering 59
Protection 60
Seeding 62
Celebration 64
Timing 65
Daily Water Aspiration Ritual 66
Common to All Rituals 67

CHAPTER 6: MEETING AT THE RIGHT PLACE 71

Background as Foreground 71
Meeting Yin and Yang 73
Yang Meetings 74
Yin Meetings 75
Eating and Meeting 77
Personalities, Meeting and Seating 79
Wealth Corner 80
All Chairs Are Not Equal 82
Table 2: Meeting Position Modifiers 83
Decision Influencers 83
Table 3: Golf Course Property Offer 84

CHAPTER 7: MEETING AT THE RIGHT TIME 87

The Law Of Correspondence 87
All Times to Meet Are Not Equal 88
Regard the Moon 89
Table 4: Rating Meeting Criticality 105
Table 5: Meeting Timing Multipliers 106

CHAPTER 8: STAGING FOR STAGING 109

Stringing Pearls Along a Cord of Awareness 110
The Fast Focus on Connecting 111
The Path to Enter and a Portal 113

Picture This 116
Staging the Near, the Far and the Attractive 118
Enter Here! 119
Wealth Corners as Positive Messages 121
Table 6: Rooms and What They Symbolize 122
What Are They Looking at Really? 123

CHAPTER 9: WHEN BUILDINGS DON'T SELL 125

CHAPTER 10: BECOMING MORE FENG SHUI REALty AWARE 141
Case History Review Journal. 146

APPENDIX 1: SOLAR AND LUNAR ECLIPSES 2015 TO 2025 152

APPENDIX 2: PLANETARY DIRECTION CHANGES 2015 TO 2025 155

GLOSSARY 163

INDEX 169

List of Tables

Table	Description	Page
1	Questions of History to Ask and Document	41
2	Meeting Position Modifiers	83
3	Golf Course Property Offer	84
4	Rating Meeting Criticality	105
5	Meeting Timing Multipliers	106
6	Rooms and What They Symbolize	122

List of Illustrations

Number	Illustration		Page
1	*Yin Yuan*, Deep Affinity	姻緣	19
2	*Feng Shui Dao*, The Way of Wind and Water	風水道	35
3	*Jia*, Family, Clan, House	家	42
4	Ritual Water Bowl		66
5	*Ichi Go Ichi E*, One Moment, One Meeting	一期一會	72
6	Meeting Room Seating		82
7	*Ming*, Brilliance, Profundity	明	89
8	*Men*, Gate, Entry, System	門	119
9	Wealth Corner Location		123
10	*Fu*, Prosperity, Divine Abundance	福	140
11	*Xin*, Heart, Mind	心	149
12	*Ryo*, Understood and Done!	了	175

INTRODUCTION

"Thirty minutes, no more. They don't want theory; they just want new ways to sell the houses that have been on the market too long. So, keep it brief. You can slip bits of philosophical stuff in later during the tour -- only if anyone asks."

This was my first introduction to Realty Feng Shui around the longest day of the year in Anchorage, Alaska. Everything in life is an experiment of some sort. This was an experiment in teaching feng shui to real estate agents. The day had been designed beginning with a lecture to set context. A very brief lecture. For instance, I thought real estate agents might want to know what feng shui is in case someone should ask them later on. The rest of the day was devoted to teaching on a home tour. I had neither previewed nor selected these homes. In a sense, the good sense of the buying public had. A realty firm sponsoring this seminar in consultation with their top sellers had selected four or five homes that had been languishing indefinitely on the market. Several of these homes had been shown to Asian buyers, specifically, Chinese, Korean, and Japanese buyers who all had rejected purchase for one reason or another. The homes were higher end so there was greater incentive to learn in order to sell.

The plan was to tour each of the selected houses. We'd assemble on the lawn or in the biggest room and go from there. If the listing agent was present, he or she discussed the main features. Since we were all there to learn something new about feng shui, especially me, the listing agent revealed the reaction of failed prospective buyers. If a buyers' agent had shown the place to a qualified purchaser who considered feng shui important criteria in buying a home, then that agent also gave a brief history of the interaction. It was all very informal.

Up to this day, I had been somewhat sensitive about my Hoosier background, born in Bloomington, Indiana and raised in the industrial northwest-most county of the Calumet region. During the tour, we had assembled in the master bedroom suite of one of the homes. The lady of the house, and co-owner, asked if she could participate in the tour and feng shui discussions at her home which the organizers and I had agreed to readily. One Alaskan realty agent asked the question: "How's their sex life?" On the whole, just about any question deserves a good answer because feng shui is about how places influence and change people's behavior. As sex life is behavior of sorts, the question deserved an answer, but not in those circumstances and, definitely not at that moment. Ever since that sunny Alaskan day in June, I have never taken the least offense at being called a Hoosier, whether in jest or as an intended insult. Hoosiers are far from last in the ways of polite society.

The method continued. We walked into each room of each house. I would discuss the feng shui room basics, then say if I thought this room were harmonious or out of balance. We considered the basic architectural layout, and we also considered how this place was staged or arranged with furniture and other decorations. In another house, in another very large master bedroom suite, with no owner/occupant present, I made the comment that the only feature that could make this room worse would be to have put a mirror or skylight above the double bed. A gasp from the back caused everyone to turn around. One real estate agent said she and her husband had just remodeled their master bedroom suite. They had wanted to include a skylight over the bed, but could not afford it. I praised their good karma of having a limited budget and moved on again, happier yet to be a Hoosier.

Along the way, we discussed many other things. My intent was to teach how awareness of feng shui might improve their sales interactions with clients, improve the future fortunes of the clients to whom they had sold homes, and, ultimately improve their own bottom line results. It was imperative for me at each house to discuss who might the better prospective buyers be from a feng shui perspective, and, secondly, how this place might be transformed into a more attractive, sellable place. Often at this point our interests diverged. The agents' interest was to sell the house as expeditiously as possible to whomever could afford it. My interests were to improve the house so that it would bring either lesser harm or greater benefit to those who would live in it later.

This brings us to the main reason we are writing this book. We do not believe that the sales event and long-term feng shui interests are irreconcilable aspects of a real estate sales transaction. In fact, in the course of pursuing your realty careers, making certain there is good feng shui present is just as important as assuring there are no termites eating away at the joists and the future wealth and happiness of its occupants. We hope to demonstrate this while also giving you many easy to use insights into feng shui.

In 2006, when we wrote the first draft of this book, it made little sense in the world of residential real estate. Houses were flying into escrow with offers far in excess of asking prices. The bursting mortgage bubble was not yet evident. Sellers and their listing agents were over-confident. Home buyers were groveling everywhere and would not consider asking for much in return during the transaction. In some volatile markets, buyers even bribed sellers despite the patent illegality of such behavior. Of course, the over-inflated market fell drastically almost taking the entire country into a desperate depression. In the aftermath, people went bankrupt, houses were sold very short, and significant abandonment of realty property was common on every block of suburban America. That especially included new houses sold in planned and badly planned developments.

Would paying attention to real estate at the feng shui level of awareness have made a difference during the sellers' market frenzy? We can't answer that at the macro-economic level. During the past decades of feng shui consultations, though, we have noticed that houses that failed -- short sales, foreclosures and abandonments, even houses physically pirated for building materials, fixtures and appliances -- all have displayed significant negative feng shui characteristics. Buyers and buyers' agents who knew of that before making an offer in an outrageous market would have reduced their liability to ultimate loss. Some fiscally overextended buyers would still have suffered a devastating loss, but the majority, in our opinion, would not have magnetized their own financial ruin. They could have weathered the unfavorable winds of the economic storm.

Beginning with the first realty seminar that we experimented in teaching, and over the course of several decades of advising on both ends of sales and purchases of houses, condos, housing developments, apartment buildings, storefronts, malls, office buildings, and manufacturing space, I've learned many things. Also, as Anita began selling houses in 1998 in Palo Alto, Phoenix, Scottsdale, Cottonwood and Prescott, our combined learning of feng shui applied to real estate sales has accelerated. This book is intended to help you also accelerate your own learning of realty feng shui.

The ideas and examples we present are from a practical point of view. We could just as easily have titled the book, *Feng Shui On the Move* because it will provide you with immediate changes you can insert into the deal that's delaying you right now. Over time, and in the normal pursuit of your realty career, this book provides enough information to give you a basic grounding in feng shui while you pursue your sales on the run. As the organizer of my first feng shui seminar advised, there is not too much philosophy here. If you are interested in more details about feng shui, we refer you to *Feng Shui: The Art and Harmony of Place* by Johndennis Govert. There are also over three hundred other English language books that can fill in more details.

We have organized the approach in this book to facilitate your immediate experimentation. What you will also find in this book, woven among the results-oriented changes you can do today, are deeper and enduring insights. These insights can gradually transform your approach from a real estate agent who knows a little about feng shui to a feng shui savvy agent whose knowledge and skill improves finances, fortunes and life satisfaction for others and for yourself.

Place, the Final Frontier

Throughout the book, you will find the word, "place" used often, starting with the title, *REALty Feng Shui: Places and Profits in the Marketplace*. Usually, place refers to some dimension described by length, height and depth. It can be plotted on a map, a plat or a globe. It can be described by the natural wonders or built world we find present at a location. Occasionally, in this book we use the word, "place" to point to a greater quality of place that is an intersection and interaction of space, time, matter, energy and intention. When we do that, and want to draw your attention to the greater, more galactic idea, you will see it printed as "place (所)." The Chinese character in parentheses is a word for place, spoken as "*suo*" in Chinese or "*tokoro*" or "*sho*" in Japanese. The character is a combined picture, a door on the left side connected to the image/idea of a unit of weight of 1.32 pounds (600 grams) on the right. The character combines a boundary sense of space that we may enter or leave joined together with a suggestion of earth density. Place, in this sense, is a dimension of our experience. Unlike space, place is grounded in the tangible and familiar.

CHAPTER 1

How Feng Shui Works

The word for word translation of "feng shui" from Chinese to English is "wind water." What feng shui refers to is a classical science and art. The science of feng shui is knowing how place (所) effects people, not just how it makes them feel, but how it actually alters their behavior. The art of feng shui is setting about changing the effects a place (所) has on people. Wind and water are a poetic description of the process. Wind refers to the subtlest effects of place (所), while water refers to the most obvious. Everywhere in between, meaning every effect from the subtlest to most obvious is of concern in the science and art of feng shui.

In the classical Chinese era (before 600 BC prior to Confucius and Lao Tzu), some of the wind effects we now face in the 21st century real estate world did not exist. There were no feng shui discussions of radon emissions, electro-magnetic fields (EMF), ambient air pollution, or toxic breezes from chemical dumps. There were plenty of other subtle effects considered like weather patterns, geologic faults, seepage, ghosts, and unusual field phenomena. Of the water effects, classical China had no nuclear test grounds, airports, chemical manufacturing plants, or vast underground sewer or train systems as under Paris or Tokyo. Yet there were other obvious effects, like mountain or river sites, neighborhoods, city zoning, and proximity to borders. And there was everything else in-between. The point is that the originators of this science and art made feng shui broad enough so that all things about place (所), discovered or yet to be discovered, would fit within its breadth.

To get a feel for feng shui, consider wind and water in another context. Whenever the weather is about to change from sunny and clear to stormy, there are signs. The first is wind change which moves the clouds into place (所). Later as the weather front approaches, wind directions shift more abruptly and the wind becomes stronger and colder. At this moment, even before water from the sky arrives as rain, sleet or snow, animal behavior changes. Our human behavior also changes. The weather condition may be a front along thousands of miles, or it may be a local effect within a few city block radius. How animals and humans move and act within the changing area is a great example of feng shui at work. The Chinese word for weather is "*tianqi*" or, "heaven's energy." So, when heaven's energy moves, to some degree, everyone moves in response. Later on, the storm may again change back to a beautiful day. Tensions are released, birds chirp. Once again human and animal behavior changes with the feng shui.

In common speech now you will hear people say: "This house has very good feng shui," or, "That room has bad feng shui." In talking like this, they are not directly referring to wind or water, but to the underlying conditions of the place that will cause good or bad effects on the people who live or work there. A new verb has even entered English and can be heard at cocktail parties: "to feng shui" or "to get feng shuied," as in: "Last week, I got my house feng shuied and I feel absolutely fabulous." You also hear: "I got feng shuied Friday and it hasn't done a thing for me."

It is a common experience for people to react to places. The extreme examples are easiest to see. We or our friends have personally experienced this. We enter a store sometime in our shopping careers, and feel overwhelmed or acutely anxious. We may even feel as if our skin is crawling, so that our reaction causes us to leave immediately. We remove ourselves from the effective field of bad feng shui and get out into the relative comfort of the street. The opposite condition happens at a party or restaurant at which someone gets so comfortable and happy that they fail to notice that it is one o'clock in the morning and their hosts are hinting and yawning. In fact, everyone else has gone home. But, because they are experiencing the positive effects of feng shui, they no longer care for the niceties of social convention and party on in bliss.

The common experiences of extreme aversion or extreme attraction to a place do not happen every day. Most places we move in and out of elicit a mixed response. You may ask your friend: "Well, how was it?" She may respond: "It was...okay," meaning that there were both some interesting and disturbing features of the place. On the whole, she has averaged it out as "okay." English does not sport a vocabulary with which you nor she can easily draw close distinctions about place (所). Chinese feng shui, on the other hand, does. The Inuit language uses many words where English uses one word, "snow." An Eskimo's survival in the northern tundra depends on correctly identifying threatening conditions of an icy landscape. Similarly, Chinese has many words and ideas for the effects of place. Because part of your career and financial health as a realty agent depends upon correctly understanding place (所) in depth, adding feng shui ideas to your dictionary of experiences can only improve your business and personal satisfaction.

For the moment, let's translate feng shui into familiar western business and scientific concepts. Real estate, whether it is undeveloped land, a house, or commercial or manufacturing building is ultimately a patterned energy field. That field exhibits power fluctuations, time cycles, and it is bound within a system of relationships. It is sound, motion and light. When we look at a house and see a static object, we are deceived. At the smallest level, every building and landscape material is a vibrating complex of sub-atomic charges. If we were able to count and sort all the charges present in a two-story Tudor estate, that information would still not tell us how the whole system worked at larger levels of scale. Practically, feng shui allows us to read the pattern of energy of places at different scales. It allows us to assess the effect it will have on one person, a family, or society at large. If we descend scales, it can tell us the effect a bedroom will have on someone's digestive system or on their checkbook by next August. Feng shui also provides us with a set of interventions we can make to change the system so that it will produce altogether different effects.

The most accurate way to consider feng shui is as the sum total of effects of everything that ever happened at or in that place (所). The building site has a history and energy for the underlying layer of the feng shui. Every building material used in the original construction or at later remodels form another layer of feng shui. Everything that the construction crew said, did or thought in making or remodeling the building is another layer of feng shui. Every thought, word and deed of the first occupant during their tenancy is another layer of feng shui. Every thought, word or deed of a guest is another layer of feng shui. Each succeeding occupants' thoughts, words and deeds over the course of their tenancy form other layers of feng shui. Each of these feng shui layers is a complex of energy events, some quite strong, some very weak. Although this scale of perception is complete, it is too massive to contemplate. Instead, there are shortcuts to gauge the dynamic pulse of place (所). We will be discussing these limited yet essential set of evaluations and fixes for feng shui effects throughout the next chapters.

How does feng shui work? That answer would require another book to consider well. Instead, how about a few provocative thoughts before we move to more practical matters. Feng shui comes from an underlying perception that every event happens because of interlocking interconnections. Groups change together as they affect one another. This contradicts the 18th century western scientific view holding that events only occur at random. It does agree with the scientific view that a number of causes act together at the same time. Experiments from quantum physics tend to support the view that underlies feng shui: everything is intricately interconnected from thought-energy to weather, from solar flares to anger. The new physics, though, has not arrived yet at all the same conclusions as feng shui.

Another view is that the universe is holographic. Each part reflects the whole. Each part is a mirror of every other part. In feng shui, your house mirrors your life. If you live in a very messy house, then undoubtedly your business and personal affairs are also in a cluttered mess. If you have all kinds of plumbing leaks, then your bank accounts are similarly leaking. If your house just started to drain lots of thermal or electric energy, then your body will drain vital energy, and you soon will get ill. Or the same condition may mean that no one in the family will spend much time at home.

When you look in a mirror and try to comb your hair, you soon see that everything works backwards. You have to make an effort to act in reverse in order to make the hair in the mirror go from right to left. There is a learning curve in feng shui too as you begin to read personal life reflected in land and buildings. You have to learn to see the link between outer feng shui actions and corresponding changes in your client's life. For instance, what happens in salesman's life when he puts world maps up on his walls? What happens to a family that puts a sidewalk from their front door not just to the driveway, but all the way to the street? What happens to the corporate president after he moves into the corner all-glass office? Once you learn to read the patterns that are prominently displayed everywhere, an entirely new world of insight and action is revealed.

For one thing, and this is a thought that should not be uttered in the presence of hungry lawyers: for whatever good comes to the occupant of real estate you sold, you are one of several causes of their good fortune. For whatever negative events occur to the occupants of buildings you have sold, then you are one of several causes of their bad fortune. Naturally, by knowing feng shui, you can help others and help yourself escape some upcoming negative events. Feng shui is not about completely fixing another's life; rather, it's about improving a building which in turn will improve their life somewhat. You've lived a good life if you've left the world better than how you found it. You will do good feng shui if you improve someone's life circumstances above the condition in which you discovered them.

Learning feng shui is not an armchair pursuit. It is an interactive, living experiment that produces sometimes immediate and unexpected results. The best way to learn is by trial and error. Then you can see how it works and prove its worth in the laboratory of your own experience. If someone asks: "Do you believe in this feng shui stuff?" You can answer: "My experience is that feng shui changes have transformed my life and improved my clients' lives too!" Then you can say: "This is what has worked well for me."

Once you get to this level of feng shui practice, it may not make you an expert, but it does make you more effective in navigating your daily life to more satisfactory shores. Who is a feng shui expert anyway but someone who is much more satisfied than the rest of humanity. While the life circumstances of others may resemble tempests that dash their hopes and their peace of mind on the rocks of chance, you can use feng shui to steer your course more swiftly, surely and harmoniously to your chosen port of call.

Let's end this discussion of how feng shui works with a few practical concerns about ownership and occupancy. Because feng shui is an energy field, it really has very little effect if you do not expose yourself to that field. So, from a feng shui perspective, ownership of place is almost irrelevant, although it is central to real estate. Who can own an energy field anyway? Rather, if you own a place that you lease, it is not you, but the occupants who are influenced most by the feng shui. If as landlord, you come by physically to collect rent, or make repairs, you are exposed directly to the feng shui only so long as you're on site. The more time you spend in a place (所), the more you become subject to its influences, whether negative or positive.

The occupant is the party most affected by a building's feng shui. The remote owner does not escape the building's feng shui effect, because he or she has tangled themselves up in the field, though less acutely. If a rental house, apartment complex or office building has feng shui that contributes to the financial collapse of its occupants, of course it will affect the owner, but only indirectly. It is in the enlightened self-interest of every owner who wants a decent financial return on real estate investment to assure that a building has minimally "solvent" feng shui, if not "prosperity" feng shui. Otherwise, the landlord will be forever dunning unlikely accounts payable and advertising frequently for a new crop of lessees. We know there are slumlords who bleed dying assets, but even slumlords have been called before the courts to account for their behavior. What catches them up is probably not the feng shui of their variously held properties, but rather the feng shui of their primary residences. Look to the primary residence of owners of many properties. There you will find the feng shui that effects the course of their private and business affairs most.

Some people are blessed (or perhaps cursed) with several homes in which they live off site and on site. They may own or rent, but what they do is migrate from place to place in the course of a year. When some event unfolds, a toothache, a 2-for-1 split of a high-tech speculative stock, or a car accident, it is largely influenced by the feng shui of where they were living at that moment in combination with their primary residence. Bi-local or tri-local living complicates understanding feng shui. As a realty agent, if you sell a family a summer cottage, you are helping them change their lives for one season every year when they vacation at that property.

Feng shui first encompasses the full range of how you think, feel, speak and act caused mainly by your physical presence in any place (所). Feng shui next encompasses the changes you make to any place to move you toward your goals. The more aware and evolved you become the less the effects of place will change you unduly. The less aware and more automatic you act, the greater will be the feng shui effects on your life for good or ill.

CHAPTER 2

Webs of Relationships

The CEO from New Zealand explained it well: "There are three aspects to every business deal, the logical, legal, and relational." He went on to explain that the core of every deal is whether the business deal is logical or sound. Do all parties profit? Can the seller furnish a quality product or service at the specified time and place? Can the buyer pay or finance it? Business logic is what primarily drives deals in Europe he said. Next there are legal considerations that protect contracting parties from unusual losses or unfair practices. The CEO said he hates doing business in the United States because too much emphasis is placed on duties, obligations and improbable outcomes. The legalistic mindset breaks more deals than it makes. The third aspect is relationship. Can the buyer trust the seller and vice versa? Do they have similar business styles and values? If they do one business deal well, why not continue to help each other profit in the future? It's easier and more efficient to continue doing business with profit-making partners by sustaining momentum than beginning each deal anew. In China, and throughout Asia, he emphasized how relationship is the most important aspect of business deals.

The CEO illustrated the relationship point with his manufacturing company's own experience in Asia. He said that for over a year he had been making marketing presentations to a Chinese firm. He moved up the corporate ladder with each encounter. For several months, he made repeated presentations and met many times with one Vice President. Finally, he made several formal and informal presentations with the company President. At the conclusion of one meeting, the President reached across the table, shook hands with the New Zealand CEO, and said: "We can do good business together." Then the President turned to his VP and asked: "What are we buying from this man anyway?" That's the difference of doing business in Asia and the West.

Feng shui, like many Asian cultural perspectives, is based on webs of relationships. There are two ways we will apply knowledge of relationships in this chapter. One is in understanding a little more deeply what the feng shui perspective is all about. The other is more practical. It has to do with establishing and nurturing relations with realty clients, some of whom are buyers, others sellers. Included are some insights for American real estate agents working with Asian clients. Finally, as more Americans embrace feng shui as an art to improve their lives, they create another market, which we will describe. Asian American real estate agents need to pay some attention to this trend because it's a reversed and often novel situation.

Feng Shui as Webs of Relationships

The feng shui of a building is not a static thing -- it's more of a moving energy connection over time. The feng shui of a house is not isolated, rather it is connected to all the houses, stores, offices, parks, roads and other spaces around it. Change enough houses in any neighborhood and you change the feng shui of a particular home. Put a four-lane highway right behind a housing development that previously had a forest, and property values dip in response. That highway, outside the control of the occupants of most homes and offices, creates large-scale negative change for home residents. The same highway creates traffic and visibility for offices, malls and retail stores and constitutes good feng shui with increased commercial property values.

This brings us to a feng shui maxim: **Harmonious feng shui is possible only by fitting in to the established building pattern.** A folk axiom in China and Japan states the same truth in a negative way: "The nail that sticks up gets the hammer."

In ancient China, knowledge of feng shui meant understanding the web of relationships in a city. Because feng shui was a shared cultural perspective, every Chinese citizen knew what were acceptable land uses in various city neighborhoods. Feng shui served as a de facto zoning plan based on developing relationships, not on law codes. Brothels were unacceptable in retail areas, the government center, or residential neighborhoods. Brothels were fine for the walled in "Willow Districts" at the edge of most towns. Part of feng shui was knowing how to fit in within the larger whole.

It did not mean submerging your personality completely like some planned use developments now seem to demand. It was very unlike land use zoning codes, especially in some areas where the maxim seems to be: "It's my land and I can do with it what I want." As a result, an inspiring church can have a five-story apartment building, a pornographic bookstore, five houses, an auto body repair shop and a Wal-Mart as neighbors. The underlying value of no zoning codes is about freedom to be inharmonious, not the feng shui of fitting in.

The ancient understanding of feng shui does not exclude innovation in lifestyle or in building development. Experimental lifestyles and experimental businesses have to occur on experimental real estate. We call these places transitional neighborhoods. Later these areas, if successful, become respectable, unique, and new patterns within the whole city. The web of the city adapts to accommodate the new. Transitional neighborhoods are always places of greatest real estate speculation. They are places to place bets on the future or invest in order to influence competing visions of the future. Following this thought one step further: transitional neighborhoods create an innovative but unstable feng shui force. At some point, if a critical mass of neighborhoods becomes transitional and unstable, the entire society will collapse in chaos. In contrast, if a critical mass of neighborhoods remains stoically static, the entire society will collapse under the dead weight of the past. Good feng shui finds a dynamic balance to sustain the web of relationships.

Client Relationships

In order to meet anyone's needs, either you have to already know those needs or learn what they are. That at least is the core of modern marketing philosophy. It still hasn't completely replaced the post-World War II sales mentality which simply is to sell what has already been produced. As a result, customers often end up with unneeded, unwanted, and unsatisfying products. This does not lead to repeat business among customers who have another choice. When real estate becomes a monopoly, buyers won't have choices and you won't have to satisfy their needs. In the meantime, work hard on relationships.

Chinese and related Asian cultures and businesses are embedded in relationships. In feng shui, you have to establish a relationship first. As you would normally do, ask what does a person, family or company want in a new place. They may say: "I want a two story, four-bedroom home, of at least 2500 square feet, with a gourmet kitchen. They may say we need 15,000 square feet of built-out office space near the airport. That information is good because it shows that the client has given the subject some thought. Unfortunately, for you it is just second hand information. It represents how they have interpreted their goals and projected them into the world of real estate. If they are very experienced in real estate, they may have projected their needs accurately. Most often, you will find that they have not very accurately translated their needs into goals, nor their goals into feasibly targeted real estate.

The main question is what does a person or company state that they want. A corporate goal might be: "We strive to maximize profits and shareholder equity over the next ten years by providing quality goods and services while ever increasing market share." For companies, this is the capitalistic pledge of allegiance. Individuals and families say: "We want to be very prosperous, healthy and happy." Neither of these statements are very good goals because they fail to focus a person or an enterprise on any important and specific activity. Most businesses or people want all those generic positives too. However, every firm and every person have a recent history of some events they want to avoid re-experiencing [1]. Sometimes they've done great things they want to repeat at a higher level. Starting with history, their goals have context. Your job is not to help them perfect things forever, but to help them find the next rung in the ladder to take the next step upward. You need to know where they are coming from and where they think they are going. You need to help them recognize the relationship between their past and the future they want to create.

Establishing a relationship is part fact finding; part sharing of your own life and business experiences, part listening to their life and business histories, part goal clarification, part market education (for you and them), and part problem solving.

---

1   Consider written contracts as legal archaeology. When an individual or corporation presents you with a first draft of a contract for your signature, many of the terms and protective covenants are no more than a litany of bad deals they have been party to over the past few years. Before you reject any of their terms out of hand, no matter how unacceptable, you may want to learn the details of how they got burned in the past. You may learn vital information that enables you to negotiate around the point, instead of breaking a deal by losing a battle over the point, all the while oblivious to a past disaster your potential business partner is desperately struggling to avoid repeating.

Integrating all these parts leads to a limited, but mutual trust for the task at hand. It also will lead to a limited but satisfactory conclusion. Another way to state the same idea is that you must allow a solution to emerge that resolves the total life impasse facing your client. The client lists a number of concerns they have. Like a shopping list of hopes, dreams, practicalities, aversions, improbabilities, and expectations, they dump their concerns on the table whether they are buying or selling real estate. You know from your own experience that not even half of these can be achieved. To be able to hear them and understand them, however, alerts you as well as the universe as to how you collectively will proceed. Relationship means allowing the collective process to be the engine driving the deal.

Relation orientation is not the way of American myth. Americans are supposed to display hustle, inventiveness, individual initiative, and can-do verve. It seems the opposite of relationship orientation. A Japanese friend who has lived in the U.S. for many years describes this cultural paradox. When he sees a typically American situation, as when someone grabs a result that serves mostly his own needs and diminishes others, he muses: "What do you expect from a society that values the person so much more than the group?" When he sees a typically Japanese situation, as when one person's positive potentials are ruined by misguided group action, he counters: "What do you expect from a society that values the group so much more than a person?" What he is pointing out is the unbalance in both approaches. There is such a thing as group wisdom. There is also such a thing as group ignorance. Relationship orientation means you will allow group wisdom to work for you.

One dictum of sales is to press for commitment now. Don't wait! Do it now! Seize this nanosecond and act! This is an important part of closing the deal. In business full of uncertainties, complexities, and sudden changes, acting quickly often substitutes for acting with wisdom. As a result, realty agents or their clients often try to force choices or completion of steps before their time. Every moment is not equal. Every wine and every act ripens in its own time. Every deal establishes its own pace despite the best and worst efforts of the parties involved.

In Chinese experience, the word "*yinyuan*" describes the background over which all relationships operate. *Yinyuan* implies an already existing affinity between two people, two families or two companies. Usually, yinyuan is considered a positive, close connection. *Yinyuan* is like a fruit, in that any connection has to reach a ripe moment. Often, the relation between husband and wife is described by *yinyuan*. No matter how intimate and close you may now be to your spouse, there was a time before you met in which you were utterly unconnected. In fact, there was only a window of time and place where you could connect. A modern marital postscript is, no matter how connected and intimate you were before the divorce, you and your ex-spouse have now fallen out of *yinyuan* on the other side. When working with Asians, if both you and they sense this *yinyuan* condition, you are in the center of the relationship zone. This doesn't happen frequently, but when it does many new possibilities open for both of your futures.

Yin Yuan is a term to describe that individuals or groups of people have relational affinity toward one another. Yin Yuan can be developed but usually grows from pre-existing affinity. In the West, it might be described as chemistry between people or groups of people.

The Generic Relationship

When a company leaves its previous offices and relocates, at the most basic level, what is occurring? When a person or family sells a house and moves into another, what is the generic transition? The company and family both are entering a new phase in their business and life experiences. No matter how hopeful the next step may seem, they are each experiencing the death of the previous era. Unless their recent history has been a study in misery, they will have some mixed feelings about the move. They are leaving behind the comfort of the known for the fear, adventure, and uncertainty of the unknown.

The closer the transition date comes, the more real the change seems. The closer the transition date approaches, the more intense are the emotions generated by the anticipated life change. **Recognize this pressure as an unusual and major life stress.** If a family or firm hasn't moved within a seven-year period, the intensity of the pressure they feel will be greater. Each previous set of seven years in which a person or firm has made no change of place multiplies the overall stress. Most people react badly to the pressure of change and make poorer decisions as a result. Some people, however, actually have an ability to function better under duress, and for that small minority, the change will invigorate them.

When the movers arrive to pack things away in boxes, the home or office is broken into unconnected pieces from which it started. It had been the context of the building coupled with the owners' functional needs, aesthetic taste and practical arrangement that connected these objects into a feeling of a whole. As the whole is dissembled and marched through the sunlight (or drizzle) toward the moving van, the owners see it for what it is – many separate items. This process is parallel to dying. As the dying person watches as each of his or her body functions, then biological systems, detach from the whole and begin to dissolve back towards the beginning, he or she is confronted by the non-solidity and truly temporary arrangement of life. This step-by-step dismemberment is difficult and increases uncertainty and stress.

The relationship with any realty client is fraught with pressure and stress. The result of which may lead to bad decision-making, and often, bad behavior whether socially or morally considered. To make the transition easier for everyone, keep reminding yourself that they (and occasionally you) are being unduly influenced by the temporary feng shui of dissolution that is acting upon and through them. Try to assess how your clients will react under stress. What are their weak and strong personality characteristics? To find out, encourage them to tell stories of their other life transitions so you will have a parallel situation or two against which to judge them. Then, you will begin to have an idea of what kind and how much counsel to offer them. You are one of their coaches responsible for moving them toward their desired future, so continue to restate and reflect their goals and dreams back to them. The more easily they can envision themselves in an improved future, the easier it will be for them to let go graciously of their present circumstances.

Advice for Sellers and Their Agents

The emphasis for a family or company who is moving is on self-dissolution so that the property and its influencing energies can be transferred to the next owner. The future cannot enter when a person barricades himself against change by maintaining the arrangement of his possessions as battlements against the unabating siege of time. The most basic ritual is emptying out. It is perhaps one of the most spiritual rituals because it requires great detachment and faith in the future in order to perform it well. Although both buyer and seller have to perform this ritual, the seller experiences greater focus on emptying the building before the new owners are able to take possession. The listing agent has to be the primary coach to clients about maintaining momentum in emptying out rituals.

On a practical feng shui note, the seller should seek to meet with the listing agent outside the home as much as possible for two reasons. The first is that as the sale gets closer to the certainty of closing, more household items are packed and the environment edges more into chaos. By meeting at an orderly, appealing place, outside the boundaries of the moving chaos, conversations, and viewpoints will be expressed more clearly and decisions executed with greater acumen and confidence. The second reason for meeting outside the house is that the sellers, by exposing themselves to a new, but appealing environment, become more open to new ideas and fresh perspectives. It is much easier to generate and sustain enthusiasm for the ordeal of a life or business transition when you focus on the positive promise of creating the future rather than dissolving the past.

"Ode on a Bungalow" Advice for Buyers and Their Agents

There are daunting numbers of legal, financial, personal and logistic details that must be addressed in purchasing a new building or undertaking a long term commercial lease. Understandably, the goal of the client is to return to business and life-as-usual as quickly as possible. There is comfort in the order of routine, even if the routine is flawed. Faced with solving all the simultaneous problems of moving, re-establishment and quickly decorating, poor decisions are the likely result because clients want to end the uncertainty much more than they want to find satisfactory solutions.

John Keats, the famous English poet, described the creative process as "negative capability." In that state, many details are unresolved, but horizons are unlimited. He reminded us that the discipline of creativity is to remain in the "negative capability" zone long enough to evolve a positive, great and complete creation. Applied to real estate transitions, encourage your clients to live with the temporary chaos of "negative capability" long enough to establish good feng shui as they create a new arrangement. It is unrealistic to expect to plan every detail in advance and become settled in a few weeks. A feng shui rule of thumb is expect to take a season to think and feel your way successfully into a new life rhythm. It takes three months to evaluate your new space from the inside, to re-arrange your old furniture and old routines, to add new furniture, art and attitudes where the old ones no longer fit.

If a home has been newly constructed and requires landscaping, it will take a full year for the household routine to settle into a normal pattern. It will take a year or longer to establish the landscape details outward from the inner core. Often homeowner association covenants require landscaping to be completed within three months, but this is an unnatural requirement because neighbors want to restrict their exposure to transition time. They too are unwilling to live with the uncertainty and creativity of "negative capability." Good advice for clients is to do only the most basic landscaping that will satisfy the letter of the law until they evolve the details after they explore and experience the possibilities of the yard. Gardens and landscaping require more time than interiors to get them right. This is because it takes longer to learn well from nature, and yard possibilities are greater in number than room possibilities.

In larger, newly-constructed commercial buildings, the amount of time it takes for the building to stabilize is two-and-a half to three-and-a-third years. The greater the area excavated, or the deeper the foundation must be dug, the longer it will take that building to settle into a stable pattern. Companies, or families that move into high-rises or big condo complexes for example, may be able to establish themselves comfortably in three months, but the outer building influences will remain off-balance and quirky. These outer and larger influences will on occasion shake the routine of the building occupants. In any case, maintain a reasonable expectation about how long it takes to establish good feng shui. Also, test this observation by asking your old clients when they achieved a functional, satisfactory re-connection of their family or work world.

Advice to Agents with Asian Clients

The default world-view of the West is a science based view with an unshakeable faith in the randomness of the universe. The feng shui perspective rooted in China's ancient past and its three main philosophical schools of Daoism, Confucianism and Buddhism, however, views all actions as resulting from previous causes in often complex webs of interrelation. Asians who want to succeed economically and socially in the worldwide emerging techno-society are not apt to admit belief in feng shui, but may secretly and selectively use it. So, there are rules for agents with Asian clients:

1. Discover the depth of your client's belief in feng shui. They may be open about it or very guarded. If you ask what features of feng shui make sense to them in relation to the property they are searching for, then you will most likely get workable information. If you discuss feng shui as a philosophy, it is likely you will reach an impasse without discovering their feng shui criteria. If you are open, you will learn their position, but if you declare a strong opinion of feng shui (for or against), you are likely to put an end to the subject.

2. Find out who within the company or family structure will give feng shui advice on this project. In families, a parent, grandparent, family friend, uncle or aunt is part of the decision-making team. In companies, the feng shui adviser may be someone who accompanies the agent in a group tour around the prospective property. You may be introduced by name, but with no hint of

what the person's expertise really is. Later, Asian clients' may choose to ignore parts of the feng shui advice, but seldom will they ignore all of it, especially if the judgment is that the overall feng shui will produce disaster.

3. The bigger the project, when Chinese banks or financiers are involved, the more critical feng shui recommendations become. At large scales, usually in commercial properties, feng shui evaluations, and the willingness of Western families or firms to follow feng shui recommendations, makes or breaks deals.

Advice to Asian Agents with Non-Asian Clients

The hemispheres are intertwining in a funny way as East and West interchange cultures. Westerners are turning to feng shui as a way to help them improve their lives, advance their business fortunes, ignite their love lives, heal their illnesses, heap wealth upon their doorsteps, and find serenity in a swirling world. The time is similar to the early 1970's when acupuncture and Chinese medicine came openly to America. Those who sought healing from the new, foreign system had illnesses not effectively treatable by Western medicines. They needed healing now, not when medical research might find a cure in forty years. Determined, they experimented with Chinese medicine. For many, lifestyles in the West are out of balance, and in this strait, feng shui holds forth hope of restoring order and activating life aspirations. As a result, Americans in larger numbers are experimenting with feng shui.

Now that Westerners are learning this science and art, there is a strange inversion. Some Westerners know far more than Asians about how, and maybe why, feng shui works. A much larger group are those who know bits and pieces gleaned from books, magazines, travels in Asia and occasional conversations. This latter group are often misinformed, and have more enthusiasm for the idea of creating harmony in their homes or offices than they have commitment to follow specific feng shui recommendations that may produce the harmony they want. For Asian agents, follow these rules:

1. Discover the depth and accuracy of your client's feng shui beliefs. You will need to discover both how much they know and how misinformed they are. They may want to discuss the general philosophy of feng shui, but you will need to pin them down to indispensable feng shui features of their ideal real estate. Getting them to identify examples of desired building features is the best way to discover how clear or confused they are.

2. Western clients often do not have anyone else in their circle to offer solid feng shui advice on their behalf. You may need to know a few feng shui consultants to recommend to them. If they are unwilling to pay for good advice, then they do not value feng shui that much.

3. If they are loosely concerned about feng shui, you don't have time to instruct them personally about feng shui but you need to do so if you are to work together. Find a few good books in English with which you are familiar in detail, then refer your clients to those books. Both of you then will have some common ground

about which to discuss feng shui concerns. If the Western client knows more about feng shui than you, ask which books most closely describe the client's approach. Then, you have to do your homework to establish the common ground.

Advice for Heirs and Estate Agents from Beyond the Pale

When heirs set out to dispose of an estate, whether in line with or against the wishes of a person who has died, the will of the person reaches from beyond the grave to influence the transition. More accurately, the life energy pattern of the deceased remains active as a drive or an obstacle to closing and redistributing the estate. There are many possible variations that effect the transaction:

- how strong or weak a personality the deceased was

- whether the death was sudden or violent, easy or difficult

- how well prepared or accepting of death the deceased was

- how orderly or chaotically, harmoniously or aggressively, the deceased lived her or his life

- how unified the executor, agents, and heirs are in carrying out the will, both intentions and literal legacy of the deceased

The main consideration is that there is an invisible hand at work in settling the estate as well as all the hands of the living actors.

By recognizing the phenomena and gauging its strength and character, agents and heirs can move through the legally protracted steps with greater ease and peace of mind. The generic task is to bring closure to the life of another person. The dissolution of the home and settling of pending affairs of the deceased truly is a continuation of the death process, only on a social, and perhaps moral level. It is fraught with greater grief, stress and impact than other transactions even when disregarding the added legal complications.

When purchasing an estate home or home office, the traces left by the previous occupant require more effort to clear. Everywhere there are unfinished threads of activity that need to be dissolved. Purification rituals, re-painting, re-carpeting and re-decorating need to be more extensive in estate sales in order to dissolve the old threads and establish the new occupants securely and harmoniously. If the estate property proves difficult to sell, market conditions aside, it means that the old energy has to be cleared more vigorously so a new party can visualize themselves happily living or working in the vacated space. Ways to accomplish this are discussed in rituals to improve the energy of buildings in Chapter 5.

CHAPTER 3

Feng Shui World Views

In the Introduction, we started a story of three Asian buyers in Anchorage who toured the same property. The house was newly constructed in a new development, over 4,000 square feet, and near the ocean. All three buyers rejected the home for feng shui reasons. Three different Asian buyers gave three different feng shui reasons for non-suitability. The listing agent wanted to know if they each cited good feng shui reasons for rejecting the house or merely invented reasons to disguise personal preferences.

The first clients were a middle-aged Chinese couple whose children were in their teens or in college. They looked at the house from the back seat of the realty agent's Cadillac, then spoke quietly in Mandarin. The husband announced the couple's conclusion that the house was not right because the front door did not face the east. They did not need to see anything more to make a better decision.

The second set of clients were a younger Chinese couple with two pre-school children. The agent showed them the entire house. The couple retraced their steps to the master bedroom where another conversation in Mandarin ensued. Again, the husband announced the couple's conclusion. He said: "My wife and I have considered how we could arrange our furniture in this room. There is no way we can place our bed so we can see the rising sun in the East when we wake. This house does not have good feng shui for us."

The third set of clients was a young, newly-wed Korean couple. The realty agent had shown them the house a few days earlier and they fell in love with it. They were anxious to buy it, but they were obliged to let the wife's grandmother, Omah, counsel them on whether or not the feng shui was good enough. Omah was also going to live with the young couple and help them care for the children that were to be born. When the realty agent pulled her Cadillac up to the curb, the newly-weds quickly exited and ran up the front walk. Omah, who needed the assistance of a cane to walk, took more time. She got out of the car, took three steps toward the house, then paused to inspect it. She turned around and got back into the car. She announced in Korean to her grandchildren that the five-step stairway at the entrance of the house would cause financial difficulties. It was bad feng shui. The dejected newly-weds instructed the agent to continue the house search.

How does this make any sense? There are two variables to consider, personal goals and systems of feng shui. In the last example, the stairs leading up to the house were shallow compared to runs of stairs you might find in Seattle or San Francisco. Maybe Omah did not want to climb any stairs. Maybe Omah reasoned from her experience that every life is filled with ups downs of all types, especially financial. If in the future, there were any extra financial obstructions, signified by the entry stairs, the couple would have to cut their lifestyle. They will not send their children back to Korea, but they may have to send Omah home to make ends meet. She doesn't want to return to Korea, and she doesn't want to inflame her arthritis by climbing steps every day, so Omah advises against this purchase. How past personal history and future goals influence feng shui is easy to see. How feng shui systems work is harder to grasp for Westerners.

Systems of Feng Shui

When three different Asian families use three different sets of feng shui standards, naturally Westerners are confused by this ambivalence. We think, either it's good or it's bad feng shui. How can it be both sometimes, and neither occasionally? Actually, there was not just one feng shui system that originated in China at just one historical moment. There are many systems that originated in succeeding eras in the vast Chinese empire over thousands of years that were exported to neighboring Asian nations. Once transferred to a new host nation, whether Vietnam, Japan or Korea for instance, as people experimented with the imported Chinese style feng shui, they modified the system to fit their culture. As a result, lots of feng shui systems with parallel and often contradictory recommendations have emerged.

Although this does not conform to Aristotelian either-or-reasoning, the bedrock of the Western worldview, nonetheless, we do navigate quite well around many competing systems in the West. For instance, consider health care. There are universities, hospitals, specialty clinics, MDs, pharmacies, drug companies, insurance corporations, and a host of related suppliers and support professions in allopathic medicine. There are practitioners of homeopathic medicine who sometimes include MDs. There are many systems of massage from sensual to therapeutic. There are practitioners of Chinese medicine, acupuncture and herbs. There are chiropractors and naturopaths with different philosophies and therapies. There is a spectrum of nutritionists who don't often agree on anything except that we should eat sensibly for better health. There are curanderos and psychic healers of every ilk. Somehow, when we ail, we choose a system and a healer that we judge as likely to heal us. If you encountered this array of options and ways to spend your money without previous knowledge of the subject, you would be overwhelmed and very skeptical. Instead of a neophyte in health care, you find yourself a neophyte in feng shui.

In general, there are three basic approaches: cultural or folk feng shui, power feng shui and feng shui dao. **Cultural feng shui** is the most group-oriented system, as in "our group versus your group." It is rooted in the Chinese language. Asian cultures like the Korean and Japanese who adopted the Chinese system of writing and adapted it to their own language also share very strong feng shui roots in their languages. Its basic premise is to maximize my family's good fortune within the context of my community while holding negative impacts to others to a minimum. Cultural feng shui is really a de facto set of zoning regulations enforced by common understanding and acceptance rather than by city planning commissions and departments.

Power feng shui is based on the art of war. Its basic premise is to maximize my advantage as I disadvantage you. Clearly, it is a win-lose system appealing more to those desiring dominance in the military, judicial, political, technological or corporate business worlds. Its rules will never be disclosed completely to outsiders – even among Asians. You may, however, be able to observe its effects in the corporate and political corridors and board rooms. Many of Chairman Mao's building projects for the masses were instances of negative power feng shui.

Finally, **feng shui dao** is based on creating harmony from moment to moment for everyone. It is as much a way (*dao*) of life as it is a science and art that seeks win-win outcomes in every place. The practice seeks to improve yourself and to improve others simultaneously. The pinnacle of this art is to understand the universe in the most sublime ways, yet give practical, positive expression in common living.

Feng Shui Dao is the Way of Wind and Water. It is at once a path of artistry and spiritual development around creating and sustaining harmony of place.

To show how these three approaches may each be used by the same person, consider the example of a female, Asian lawyer. The system used depends upon life circumstance as much as it does life goals. In her work, the lawyer will use every bit of power feng shui she knows to establish and manipulate her success. In her home life, she will want to create the best life for her family and will use whatever cultural feng shui she can. Her more knowledgeable friends and relatives will advise her, with or without her asking for their input. Maybe, later in her retirement, or as a result of studying brush painting, she will pursue a path to personal peace, and will now use *feng shui dao* as the most suitable philosophy by which to arrange her place and her life.

There are two schools of feng shui usually discussed, but really there are four different emphases in feng shui systems. **Form feng shui** analyzes the shapes of land, watercourses, buildings and rooms. It looks at how building and landscape shapes effect our lives. It shows how we can work with these shapes to fashion a better future. **Cosmological feng shui** analyzes the correspondence between astronomical phenomena, cosmological philosophy, and the flow of our daily lives. Most difficult to understand for Westerners who have little or no prior knowledge of Chinese astrology or philosophy, cosmological feng shui has perhaps the greatest amount of sub-systems, often very contradictory in their conclusions. Both Form and Cosmological feng shui are considered schools.

There is a third emphasis, **symbol feng shui**. This system focuses on analyzing the symbols (pictures, dreams, artwork, omens, everyday objects) with which people surround themselves. Through symbolic behavior (rituals) or through changing the symbols in a place, you can create more harmonious feng shui. Lastly, **energetic feng shui** analyzes *qi* (a life energy) and the entire spectra of energies that move in and around a place that influences the outcome of actions. By changing the local patterns of energy, you change the events that happen to the occupants of any home, office, campground, store, mall or housing development.

It's All Relative

In viewing all the feng shui systems and personal viewpoints, you need to keep in mind that feng shui is relative. There is no absolutely good or bad feng shui. It is like yin and yang, dark and light. These two are always in relation to one another. There is no absolute yin without reference to yang; and there is no absolute yang without reference to yin. This is illustrated in the *taiji*, the circle that shows yin and yang as phases of the same cycle. As one diminishes, the other increases to a turning point. Then, yin and yang move in reverse relation till the next turning point and the next change of direction. Everything is connected to its opposite, and feeds on its opposite.

Practically this means that one set of feng shui solutions is not good for everyone in every situation. The variables of their temperament, social status, life stage, health, and present circumstances must be accounted for. The number of people living or working in a place is a major determinant of the feng shui problems and ultimate resolutions. Finally, the goals, dreams and life values that individuals, families or firms pursue are very different. To support the particular goals, human personalities, and land and building configurations, the "optimal" feng shui arrangement is ever different.

CHAPTER 4

Learn from History

One of the primary, and incidentally, fastest ways to evaluate the feng shui of a residence or office is to get as detailed a history as possible about previous tenants. Because feng shui effects those who are exposed to the energy field of the building, it is the occupants who are effected most rather than property titleholders. The history of the tenants who may be owners provides an outline of how the feng shui of this property has influenced a person or company, and so most likely will influence the next occupants in a similar way. Therefore, the first order of business is to find out everything that you can about what has happened. By researching history, you are in fact detailing with great clarity who the next buyer/occupants will most likely be. If you are an owner or listing agent, these past tenant descriptions form the bull's eye of your potential target market.

What you will learn from this history are certain demographic facts, like age, income range, family size, education, occupation, maybe company affiliation, and certainly, financial capability. Of course, these pieces of information realty agents automatically research. What you will also learn are many other patterns. You may not be able to advertise in a targeted media to people who match these patterns, or have the potential to match these patterns in their lives, but when you do meet them, you will be able to recognize them immediately. This will give you great insight as to who are really the most qualified prospects by all the usual realty standards and by feng shui affinity as well. Feng shui affinity reveals who are most likely to move into the house or office and fit easily into the pre-existing pattern. When you hear potential buyer/occupants discuss massive renovation or redecoration plans, you are hearing people who do not want to fit themselves precisely into the underlying pattern. This is a good conversation to overhear, especially if there had been one, or a series of negative events associated with that place.

Table 1: Questions of History to Ask and Document

Topic	Residences	Businesses
Identity	Who's lived there?	Type of Business
Size	Family or household size	Number of Employees
Income	Who earned how much?	Annual revenue growth
Spending Pattern	Common and unusual expenses & trends	3 to 7 main categories of expenditure & trends
Community Relations	Activity in community groups & neighbor relations	Activity in merchant, civic, or professional associations
Education	Children's schooling through adult education	Training programs, internal or customer seminars
Commuting	Car reliance, driving distances & patterns	Local vs. national or international business
Group Composition	Children, parents, or any household change	Layoffs, new employees or departments
Building Changes	Renovations & interior design changes	Additions or major rearrangements
Entertainment	Parties or guest pattern	Fun events or formality
Creativity	Any artists	Company innovations
Servers	Any nannies, gardeners or household help	Employee relations & development
Health	Any major illnesses or special health regimens	Sick days, accident record
Partnerships	Marriage, relationships	Business or project partners
Wealth: Growth or Decline	Change in wealth, and unusual insurance, estate, investment shifts	Stock performance, change in investments, insurance
Deaths	Of any household member, especially from violence or prolonged illnesses like cancer	Of any business line, layoffs, or real deaths of employees or investors
Culture/Law	Philosophy, travel, professional education, legal cases	Export/Import activity, Professional affiliations, Legal cases
Success	Career path & fame	Overall success & company name recognition
Anything Unusual	Out of the ordinary	Out of the ordinary

Once you know the history of what events happened and when, you have more pieces of the life puzzle. Match the scale and timing of changes made in and around the house to the magnitude and timing of what happened in the lives of the building occupants. You may even get insights from changes in the larger neighborhood correlated to the occupants' life stories. In feng shui, these events are viewed as interconnected, never random. Once you can connect personal history to environmental change you will be able to discover many patterns that are really at work driving all our lives. What you will find are positive and negative patterns that are fascinating and perhaps unnerving.

Following is a discussion of the most commonly repeated historical patterns, including some indication of how the past event may be crucial to new buyer/occupants. These many patterns can be thought of more simply first. There is a creation energy that brings forth

Jia has a range of meanings. It can refer to family, to a school of thought, to an established business or to a physical house. It represents the larger collective in the web of relationships.

products, ideas, art, children and innovation. There is a maintaining energy that supports growth and development that connects and reconnects people and events. Finally, there is a disruption or dissolution energy that reduces and finally eliminates whatever had been placed under its influence. These three energies form a life cycle: creation, sustenance, and dissolution. A home or office usually won't just contain one of these energies exclusively. Rather, the place will dissolve some things, create others and maintain yet others. What you have to do is sort out the rooms or areas of the building and property where one or another of these energies predominates.

Marriage and partnership: There are places that connect people or groups together. The question is whether it was of long duration or only for a short moment? Next, does the alliance produce anything of value to the house dwellers that has continued forward? Finally, was the relationship the biggest event that happened in that house, or just one of the many that followed after?

Moving for success: Pushing its occupants up the business or personal success ladder is what some places do. How high the occupants go up and how quickly they achieve that success are the variables. If you can, compare the ambition for success to the results of the previous owner. Though the place was good, or possibly great, there are those who will still be disappointed that their ambitions were but partly fulfilled.

Birth of children, products, ideas: Couples who are looking to begin a family or who are having trouble conceiving and bearing healthy children will be interested in a house with fertile feng shui. If a very large number of children were born previously while there, or if only one was born, that effect can match specific family size goals. Similarly, firms that had developed a number of innovative products or services while in a building are a great promise of innovation for the next firm. But, were those products successfully marketed?

Success of children or employees: Somewhere in the eighteen years of rearing children in a house, find out how well they did academically, socially, in sports, in artistic or personal development, or in preparation for a career. That is more important to know than the quality of the school district in which the house lies. A business may have a track record of its employees moving on to greater success later because they acquired valuable skills or knowledge on the job. Whether or not the previous business retained the staff it developed is a connected feng shui concern.

Long occupancy: If the family or business remained in the same building for a long time, it is an indicator of how flexible and nurturing the energy of the place is. This is a good place only for a business or family who is looking to settle in and put down roots. For the ambitious executive whose company is international and moves its employees around, this type of home or office might become an impediment.

Extended family: Parents, in-laws, cousins, or non-relatives sometimes join and live in a household. Occasionally, children and their spouses and children move back in. And out again. If this has happened, then a similar gathering and enlargement of the household will very likely take place. The question is whether the household swells temporarily while the long-term guests find an independent place, or if they integrate together into one family, intentional or otherwise.

Sickness: There are two types of illness histories that need to be identified. The first is a chronic or recurring illness that diminishes one or more of the occupants. That pattern can co-cause anything from a minor to a major impediment in their living. The second are fatal diseases which we'll consider in the next section. If a terminally sick person moves out of the house before he or she dies, it may indicate that the place causes debilitation, but not death. The earlier that such a person moved out shows the next occupant how difficult or easily this energy can be repaired. With health, the underlying question is whether just one or more of the inhabitants experience a decrease of energy or vitality while living in that house. Especially pay attention to previous occupants who were in good health until they moved into that building. This is as true of offices as it is of homes. Since 1984, the World Health Organization has recognized that some buildings have "Sick Building Syndrome" and are carriers of ill health.

Death & other endings: If the previous occupants had lived long lives, but died while living in a house, that is not a serious problem. The fact that they had lived a long life is more to the point. If the deaths are the result of sudden violence (murder, suicide, accidents), or of long and painful illnesses, then that alerts us to a grave difficulty present. The younger the person who died, or the more unexpected the death, then the more difficult the problem is to remedy from a feng shui perspective. There are not many happy or moral uses a house like this can be put to without first fixing the condition. In a house where someone has died, it is important to find out all the other things that have also happened there, especially the positive outcomes. This will indicate where changes can be made using the underlying positive strengths of the property.

In an office setting, someone may die during the course of employment with the company. How important that person's work was to the company's success indicates the seriousness of fixing the office the deceased had occupied. In companies, "deaths" are also employee firings, layoffs or voluntary job changes. If you are part of the rank and file, beware of the office in which several staff have been fired. If you're management and dealing with a problem employee that you'd rather have resign than discharge, you will want to identify all your "ejector" offices.

Divorce: Consider divorce not just as a legal settlement to marriage, but also as an energy that ends relationships or partnerships. In divorce houses, pay special attention to the master bedroom. Sometimes the new occupants can avoid relationship disaster if they occupy another bedroom while they remodel the master bedroom suite. If a couple with a shaky relationship moves into a house like this, they will more than likely separate. If a couple has a very good relationship, the house will test them. Usually though, a happy couple will not be all that drawn to a divorce house. There are a small number of situations where one or both of the parties are seeking to end the relationship. In that case, the house, as it is, constitutes good feng shui for them.

Bankruptcy: Properties that have reverted to financiers are a big problem. Although the next owner may buy the building at a discount, the purchaser is really making the down payment on subsequent financial disaster. If the history was one of sudden and dramatic loss, then few people will gain any benefit from the property. If the loss was long and slow, that at least gives some time for the new occupants to remodel to remove the negativity. The new owners should expect that the total investment will require more money than they initially budgeted. They should also calculate that they will need to hold on to the property for a longer than average market time in order to turn the property to any real profit when they sell.

Travel: Some homes and offices literally expel their occupants. They may make frequent local road trips or maybe longer travel excursions. The commercial traveler who spends more than 50% of his or her time on the road is not much different in time at home (primary legal residence) than snowbirds who disappear for the warmth of half the year. The feng shui question is whether the travel is satisfying and/or profitable, or whether it is tedious and productive of loss.

Entertainment: Any history of frequent dinner parties with revolving out-of-town guests indicates an excess of entertainment energy. The question is whether these entertainments proved largely enjoyable and inspiring, or whether they formed a series of tiresome obligations. Another question is whether the partiers were a natural extension of the occupants' social life, or a completely non-connected group activity.

Creativity and art: Some houses have workshops, hobby rooms, studies, music rooms or art studios. The presence of these types of rooms doesn't show much more than an intent to be creative. The question is whether the occupants actually played music, created art works, wrote journals, articles or books, joined in stage productions, or actually expressed their creativity while living in the space. Some creative people may have produced all kinds of works during the era they lived at a particular house, but did so mostly at their office or in another building.

Home office: More and more people conduct a part of their career, salaried or part-time, from home. The question is how successful are they at the part of the job being performed at home? The question is most important to entrepreneurs who are using their home office as the primary place from which to launch a new business or career.

Community involvement: Whether it's a neighborhood organization, church group, the PTA, or a professional association, some people are very involved in community activities. If the previous occupants engaged in an unusual amount of civic activity, it indicates a strong, outgoing feng shui force. Questions to ask are whether their community activity increased or decreased since moving into their house. Also of importance is whether their lives were enriched, not very effected, or depleted by all their social activity.

Philosophy, religion or paradigm shift: While living there, have any of the past occupants changed their politics, religion or lifestyle? Such a major shift in worldview, whether sudden or over time, indicates a very strong feng shui force that is often overlooked. If a member of the household made such a change, was it in harmony with the others who lived there or did it cause discord? Later, did others living there make the same change of worldview? Or, did household religious, political or lifestyle choices result in an unsettled, uneasy truce?

Retreat and retire: Some homes really function like retreat centers. This is not true for very long for businesses that are not in the retreat business. When past occupants have withdrawn from their former social or business activities and kept mostly to themselves, it shows that the place has a very introspective focus. The introspection can lead to loneliness, death, artistic creation, or a philosophic shift or breakthrough. In Asia, the presumption has been that the last quarter of life ought to be dedicated fully to the pursuit of religious, artistic, philosophic or yogic accomplishments. As such, this type of house would have superlative feng shui for completing one's life cycle well.

The Best Market Research

By investigating the history of the place in detail, you will gain insight into the feng shui value of any piece of previously occupied real estate. If you are the listing agent, you will obtain a very detailed description of who the most likely prospects are. For instance, if you receive multiple offers on your client's place, you will be able to see very clearly which parties among the group are the most drawn by affinity to the property. Even in an uneven bidding contest, those potential buyers who have this shared affinity with your client have the advantage in acquiring the property, not so much because of economics, but because of a shared resonance of life patterns: your clients' past matching the buyers' future.

If you are an agent representing a buyer, in addition to advising your client of the economic value of the real estate, you will be able to determine if its feng shui value diminishes or increases its perceived value to your client. For instance, consider the case of a childless couple who really want children. They are considering two different purchase options, both are comparable, three bedroom townhomes of about the same asking price, one property on Poplar Street and another on Willow Street. While living on Poplar, the previous owners, a young couple, had two healthy children. The couple who lived on Willow however, had no children and were moving because of divorce. If the buying couple are convinced of the feng shui value of the Poplar Street home because it introduces a force supportive of their chances of having children, they might pay more for that house. How much more depends on so many subjective factors, especially the importance of starting a family to them. Conversely, because of the negative feng shui value of the Willow property, the buying couple should make no offer on that property. Living there would only introduce a force that is injurious not just to their goal of children, but to their very relationship as well.

Whether you represent the seller or buyer, by knowing the history of a difficult place, you will know that to move it expeditiously and harmoniously, you will have to convince one of the parties to change it. The change, which can include rituals and remodels (see Chapters 5 and 9), is to decrease or remove the negative influence that the next buyer does not want to encounter as an active force influencing their lives. Neutralizing a negative history doesn't need to happen on all houses or offices. In cases, though, where normal marketing isn't working, look to the history to pinpoint where the resistance is and what needs to be removed.

Mixed Life and Business Patterns

When three previous pairs of occupants of a home have divorced, but the fourth didn't, something has changed. Will the next couple, divorce or move on happily through life together? Look to two likely causes for this change of pattern: building life cycle or major remodeling. As with all created things, buildings go through cycles and finally dissolve. The duration of the path from creation to dissolution depends on many factors, but all you need to identify is if the building has changed phases. The easiest to recognize is the transition to an aged, outdated, or neglected building. Like the plumbing and electrical fixtures in such a place, the life patterns of the latest occupants don't work the way they used to. Also, easy to identify is any history of remodeling. The remodeling can involve one wing of the house that re-energizes a part of the occupants' life pattern, or it may change the entire pattern as when entire electrical, heating, roofing, plumbing, windows or insulation systems are upgraded. Don't overlook major changes to the gardening or landscaping of a building as a cause for a change in life histories.

Because a place has been remodeled, do not assume that the change has produced an automatic improvement. The history will tell you the magnitude of the change, and whether the change was negative or positive. In buildings where remodeling disturbs the balance or symmetry of shapes and energies, a formerly spectacular home may become ordinary; or, an ordinary home, may become a nightmare. By paying attention to the histories of people and buildings you can learn much more quickly in retrospect how feng shui actually works. Knowing enough case histories will make it at least eighty percent more likely that you can identify good, bad or indifferent feng shui in advance for yourself and your clients.

> Ownership is living in a place (所) for any amount of time; real ownership is living in that space with awareness. Perfect ownership is letting your awareness be fully in any place (所) you occupy. How wonderful to enjoy where you are! How wonderful to move on without a trace!

CHAPTER 5

Accelerating the Whole Sale

The moment a home or business owner decides to sell, the process becomes driven by expectations, hopes and dreams, bounded by covenants, inspections, repairs, financing, deadlines and deeds, and conducted according to standard realty practices amid uncertainty. For seller and buyer, all this is measured subjectively in their own private experiences that may exceed average transactions in ease or difficulty. There is a time element measured in speed of sale offer and speed of closure. The seller wants a quick sale so he can move on. The buyer wants enough time to satisfy herself she knows the market prices and products well, and upon making an offer, has enough time to check the property prudently. After that, the seller wants to slow down so he can move the household furnishings out while the buyer wants in as soon as possible to avoid paying on two properties. Who is accelerating and who is braking can switch back and forth many times between buyer and seller during the course of a single transaction.

Accelerating a sale has a time dimension and an experience dimension. All parties can measure time on their calendars and clocks. The best times from listing to closing are not always the fastest, especially if the transaction fails to solve lingering, irksome issues over months or years. An expeditious sale has the quality of being easier on all parties and agents involved. For all the transaction steps to unfold with ease and speed, everyone involved must be ready. Although you may not be able to control financiers, zoning officers, inspectors, title companies, repairmen, movers, or the host of other possible characters directly, feng shui can create a hub of harmonious intent that will draw these various influencers to resonate positively so they will contribute their energy to the process at the right moment.

The next several chapters give feng shui advice about how to accelerate both time and readiness aspects of the whole sale. We will discuss rituals of change, feng shui meeting management, special cases you might encounter, house staging, and the realty agent seller toolbox to make fast feng shui fixes.

Rituals That Create Wanted Change

In our secular, scientific world, we don't discuss rituals outside of church or sports where they're known as sacraments or superstitions. Consider however, that any action a person takes with intent to accomplish a result is a ritual. The more symbolic and the less direct, the more an action may seem like a ritual. At the heart though, a ritual is any act in which you express your intention and reach toward the desired result, whether that intention is subconscious and automatic or very deliberate and quite conscious. Rituals are very natural ways we harness outcomes involving resources, symbols, energies and thought forms that arise first in the mind.

Since there are three phases of activity, creating, sustaining, and dissolving followed by rest, we'll discuss rituals using these categories. Sellers and buyers are not much involved in sustaining a dream or situation by gradual adaptation, rather they are primarily involved in ending one life and beginning another. They will be dissolving an old pattern while creating a new one. If they fail to dissolve the old pattern, they will not be ready for the creation of a new one. If they fail to dissolve the old pattern sufficiently, they will only cause more disharmony and dissatisfaction for themselves and all others in the realty transaction because their minds and hearts are unprepared.

Emptying as Dissolution

Each of us can only carry forward a limited amount. What we carry forward should be relevant to actualizing our next phase of life goals. In a very physical way, a person considering a change of residence or a company considering a new office needs to remove unneeded things from their immediate living or working environments so it doesn't hinder the new unfoldment. Most people wait to the last moment when it's too late to use any judgment. Often, they will move everything they have and immediately begin a new cycle to acquire what they need to survive or thrive in the new environment. Many possessions go into the garage or storage. While it is true that in moving into a new place you may not be able to exactly know all you will need or not need from your past, nonetheless, there are things you already know are quite irrelevant. Get rid of that group of belongings so the gravity of ownership of the unnecessary doesn't pull you down.

This emptying ritual looks very much like any spring cleaning. It is completely within everyone's experience. In fact, it's so normal, it's overlooked as a ritual. The essence of this ritual is to rid yourself of the negative parts of your past so that you can move forward easily. There are several variations that make it seem more a ritual and less like a chore for seemingly the longest lasting weekend of your life. You may want to add these aspects to the emptying ritual.

1. Before you start, review why you are moving. Make it clear to yourself, your family or your company what the positive horizons of your future are. Make the vision of the future as clear as you can in your mind. If the future is too hazy, find a poster size picture of what the new change may look like. Put the picture up and view it during the period of your cleaning out whenever you casually pass it. Remind yourself that you are reaching for better living.

2. Although we may think we own things, their form and function are on loan from the earth. Sort items you are ridding into categories to sell, to pass along as gifts, or to recycle. As you put unneeded things into their respective piles, be thankful for the role they played in your life.

3. Giving the items you no longer need to others who can benefit from them creates a positive energy. The northwest coast Indians

performed this ritual at a Potlatch party. It is as efficient as it is festive as everyone invited can walk away with their own treasures and you don't have to deliver them. An open house type of party can also give you time to reminisce about your shared history. This reminiscence can help you understand and let go of difficulties while positively reinforcing the good that you have accomplished.

4. For legal purposes, some contracts use the term, "broom clean," to describe the acceptable state of cleanliness to be passed on to new tenants or owners. For those leaving however, a very thorough cleaning is meant not just to remove dirt, but to remove your own subtle attachments to the past you are leaving. The ritual is meant to remove all negative traces from the era during which you lived at a particular home or worked at a particular office. The more thorough you are at cleaning with the intention of clearing your past, the less negative impulses you will carry forward into the next phase of life.

5. When all the removal and cleaning have been accomplished, take a moment to let go of the past and move to the vision of the future that will nurture you. Some people leave gifts for the new owners, the neighbors, the animals around and to the place (所) itself to conclude their connection with gratitude.

Finally, if something very difficult, like an untimely or violent death has occurred in the place, consider bringing in a priest, psychic, or a shaman. Get the help of someone you respect outside your workgroup or family who understands the nature of what has happened and who can help dissolve the subtle but persistent emotional, thought and energy attachments you may have toward the place. The purpose of the ritual is to help you let go completely of the past so you are eager, open and free to enter your next life phase.

Creation Rituals

Before you move into a new space, take the time to make certain that it is clean and clear. The party who has just moved out of the place may not have been as careful as you in clearing and dissolving the unnecessary or painful past. The cleaning also includes the important detail of clearing the air. The feng or wind part of feng shui means paying attention to the subtle triggers of behavior. Because smell and appetite are so interconnected, don't neglect the importance of smell in effecting behavior. Yet even more subtle in the air is energy for us living beings. When we inspire, with the energies and atmospheric gases, we also breathe in secondary connections and subtle currents into our bodies. This profoundly affects us because we continually breathe.

Clearing the Air

Clearing the air firstly means removing sources of bad smells, like mold, or stale or rotting odors. Next it means renewing the air. The situation is similar to shopping for perfumes. After smelling more than a few, you can't distinguish other scents well, so you have to clear your sense of smell. Usually, you smell some coffee beans. If you were sampling many different foods, you might eat an apple slice. The acid in the coffee or apple clears the lingering scents so you can re-experience other smells or tastes with renewed sensitivity. Similarly, when cleaning, use soaps, solvents and polishes with some citrus base to clean. Then create and use an aerosol spray of an essential citrus oil diluted in water to clear the air. Finally, set out potpourris, or burn high quality scented candles or incense to create a new quality to the air. The main guide amid a million aroma therapy variations is not to use more than three different scents so as not to confuse the nose, heart and mind. Sandalwood, cinnamon or wood aloes incenses can create a calm feeling. If you burn them frequently while making a positive affirmation each time, it will begin to create a patina of calm and positivity that remains in the air for all to breathe.

Centering

Even amidst the chaos of moving in, there needs to be a center of focus that is relatively devoid of clutter. This area can contain a table and chairs, where you can gather and meet a little aloof from the riot of boxes and randomly abandoned furniture pieces. The area should contain a small table with a few symbols of the life vision you're trying to enact in your next, new life phase. The symbol of your goal can be a sculpture or a picture. The table is an altar of connection to your highest aspirations. If you are religiously oriented, it can contain statues, icons, or other religious symbols. It should contain something beautiful and alive like a plant, fresh flowers, crystals, or a small fountain of running water. The purpose of this ritual is to carve out a temporary zone of order while you move in. A larger, longer term purpose of this ritual is to keep you focused on the better and higher reasons you have moved.

Protection

If a home or business has been vandalized or was the site of a robbery, it is best to do a protection ritual after cleaning and clearing, but before the seeding ritual. The rational action is to repair fences or broken down areas that allowed the intrusion in the first place. The ritual actions are to place guardians around the house. A guardian symbol is a pair of *fu* dogs or dragon dogs placed outside the front entrance. A Western symbol might be a pair of lions or an archangel such as Michael, who wields a sword. Sometimes, Chinese buildings have a picture or sculpture of General Kwan, a great warrior, astride a fierce tiger that you encounter as you enter the front door. Similarly, any mythical warrior who powerfully protects is a good symbol substitute. Another symbol alternative is a statue or picture of a wrathful deity or Buddha placed inside the foyer facing visitors to ward off negativity and evil intent. In choosing a protector, the symbol has to have meaning for you. It might be a shield that contains the family crest and invokes the heroes of your family lineage.

If a building has been breached by a criminal, then that spot must receive some special attention because it is a weak link in the integrity of the building's energy field. You can place an eight-sided mirror or a mirror surrounded by the eight I Ching trigrams (*ba gua*) facing out at that spot. Similarly, place a *ba gua* mirror above your front door outside and facing visitors. Where the breach has occurred, you can also place a protective talisman to increase the protective energy. In order to activate the protection even further, paint three red dots on the open edge of the window or door where the building has been weak. If you live or work in a dangerous neighborhood, then you will have to paint three red dots on the edge of every window and entry door, including garage doors. Also, energize the *fu* dogs or lions at the entry by painting their eyes red. If you want to intensify this ritual, paint red on Tuesday, the day of Mars, the fiery planet.

If something very violent has happened in the building or on the grounds, like a murder or suicide, or if there have been repeated violent robberies resulting in injury, it is really best to engage a priest, lama, or shaman to perform rituals to cleanse the area and to re-establish protection. Because this is a serious and persistent matter, get the assistance of someone who has purified the lasting traces of these types of violence before. As they go about their preparation and rituals, ask what they perceive before they begin and after they complete the ritual. Also, ask if they will teach you protection prayers and rituals that you can perform daily or weekly, like a wrathful deity or fire puja, to extend and renew the protective force field around your building. Once the building is safe, you can then perform the seeding ritual.

Seeding

In cultivating any crop you wish to grow, you need to prepare the ground, which you have already done in the cleaning and clearing rituals. Like farming, you next must also seed your life hopes into the home or business building in which you are just now living or working. For this next step, on your altar, place water, candles, rice, fruits, flowers, and the symbols of your goals from the centering ritual. You will also need to write out your top three goals. Likewise, each member of the family or business unit should write their top three goals. If time allows, write the goals out three days before the seeding ceremony and read them to yourself three or more times a day.

Pick a time for the ritual when you are unhurried and comfortable. Then follow these steps:

1. Take a few minutes to relax, then meditate so your mind state is clear and empty. If prayer is your practice, pray for clarity, calm, and love.

2. Begin the ritual by reading your goals to yourself one more time. Fold the goal papers then place them in the metal bowl on the altar you have already created. You may wish to share your goals with the others in your family or keep them in your own mind only.

3. Take the bowl of rice, and sprinkle a few grains along the interior of your household, along the walls of rooms that are boundary walls with the outside. Next, go outside and sprinkle rice grains along the entire outside perimeter of the building. Finally, sprinkle rice grains along the property boundaries. As you plant the grains, keep your mind relaxed and focused on your goals. As you sow the rice grains, remember that each grain is a good deed with many great returns to you. You may wish to recite a mantra or prayer if you find that your mind wanders. AUM MONI POMO LUNG HUNG is our teacher, Master Quan's version of the mantra, AUM MANI PADME HUNG! It means "Hail to the Jewel in the Lotus!" This mantra invokes *Avalokiteshvara*, Bodhisattva of Compassion as well as activates one's own great, inner compassion.

4. Next, take a bowl of water and sprinkle it around all the places you have previously sprinkled the rice grains: the inside boundary walls, the outside building walls, and the property boundaries.

5. Next take a candle and bell or drum along as you make the same three boundary circuits. The rice grain is your goal seed and the water is the nourisher of life. Sound is the great awakener, and, fire the inspiring light force. The mantra of the Buddha of Limitless Light is AUM AMIDEWA HRI. Master Quan's version is AUM OH MAY DOE BU SUI. This mantra invokes you to radiate your own, great inner light.

6. Return to the altar, and burn the paper containing your main goals in a metal bowl to release them to the universe.

7. After this, take some of the fruit and some refreshing drink. The participants in the ritual may want to discuss ideas, sensations or intuitions each had while participating in the ritual. You may learn important information about the manner in which your goals are about to unfold. Remember that anything that seems to happen by chance during a ritual is part of the expression, and hints at the fulfillment.

You may do the ritual yourself, or you may wish to ask someone you regard as a positive person to help you. At this time or afterward, you may also want to invite a priest or shaman in whom you have confidence to bless your home.

Celebration

After you are comfortably moved in and somewhat (though not completely) settled, it is important to hold a house warming party to celebrate this new venture amid family, friends, colleagues, co-workers, clients, suppliers or neighbors. The ritual intent is to invite helpful people into your home or business as your honored guests. They bring with them their good will and friendship and bless your house or enterprise with their company. It is important to share a good meal with them, some music, laughter, and good conversation. It is important for you to talk about your goals to the people you invite. Even if you do not speak in great detail with everyone at your party, the main thing is that you are making an announcement to the community as to what your hopes and goals are. You could consider it the celebration as the concluding part of your seeding ritual. In fact, if you have any blessed fruits or grains left from that ritual, serve them to yourself and your guests as part of the meal to intensify the seeding ritual.

Timing

There are many factors you can consider as to when to perform each of these rituals. If you want all the details, contact an astrologer who can calculate the best time to perform rituals. In general, though, observe the movement of the moon. When the moon is decreasing or waning, it is usually good to do the cleaning and clearing rituals because the completion of the moon's cycle moves toward an end. In removing negative traces from your home or office, you want them to end, so you tie them to a completing cycle in nature. When the moon is new or is moving to full, perform the seeding and celebration rituals. The increasing moon cycle adds its energy to increase your goals and connections among the people who can help you. If you happen to move at the beginning of a season and link it to the right moon phase, it will increase the efficacy of the rituals that you perform even more. There is more information about timing in the following chapter.

Daily Water Aspiration Ritual

A very powerful and simple daily ritual will continue to increase the benefit of your house blessing. Fill a bowl with water. The bowl should be one that you like because of its energy and appeal. Walk outside to a comfortable place on your property. Hold the bowl at your heart level and speak your large goals for the next several years. The water will take a snapshot of the infinity of space. Your breath and your words will stir the water surface and connect with the infinity of possibilities that there are to fulfill your great aspirations. Place the full bowl in one of your wealth corners. The next day, empty the bowl by watering and nurturing your indoor or outdoor plants. Fill the bowl with water again and speak your truth to the sky. This works for everyday life, but especially if you are trying to sell your house or someone else's. Keep performing the ritual and watch as your goals manifest more easily as life events.

A **Water Bowl for Rituals** is a receptacle for your intentions that provides you with a visual reminder to nurture your goals every day. You should enjoy the bowl shape, size and color and be inspired by its artistry. The positive emotion you feel in appreciating the bowl can carry you more easily to your envisioned future.

Common to All Rituals

To conclude this discussion of rituals, there are a few elements common to all. A ritual is a creative act of projection. Generally, a ritual establishes an intention and broadcasts this intention energy outwardly. The more relaxed yet attentive the body, emotions and mind are during a ritual, the greater the intensity of the outward broadcast. The universe will respond to the outward broadcast, or so it seems. Actually, the ritual act helps us tune more easily to the corresponding vibrations of opportunities already in the world around us that can fulfill our intentions. In a sense, it becomes easier for us to encounter opportunities to fulfill our goals.

There are ways to intensify ritual energy by appealing to the senses and the sub-conscious mind simultaneously. If you create an altar, you are creating a foundation for your goals. By placing representations of the five elements on the altar (water, fire, wood, metal and earth) you are placing the building blocks of life at your disposal as a ready means for you to succeed in recombining these elements into your heart's desire as you broadcast your intention. Flowers on the altar act as lights in the dream realm to move your intents upward. If you place a representation of the highest form of a Buddha or divine being on the altar you link your request with the highest benefit for all sentient beings as you fulfill your goal. By sounding bells or drums, or by praying or chanting, you focus more deeply into the rhythm of the moment and your creative projection into place (所). By offering flowers, fruit, incense, water, sweets and other pleasant oblations on the altar, you establish intimacy, gratitude, harmony and respect as the basis for your request to the universe and its powers to fulfill your goals.

Rituals increase in intensity through repetition. So, if you maintain an altar in your home or business, you have a place of connection where you can renew the broadcasting of your intentions and requests. There are so many daily prayer and puja rituals to choose from that you should use one that is in the tradition of your religious, philosophical or mystical experience. At the end of whatever daily prayer or meditation ritual you practice, renew your goals and release them to the universe again. Daily practice allows you to tune the energy intent, amplitude and tone of your goals as you move toward their rapid and harmonious completion.

The final and perhaps most subtle consideration is how to perform a ritual. On one end of the spectrum, when you project your goals into the higher and lighter realms of the universe, you can specify exactly and in great detail how you expect your goal to become realized. This is ritual with content. The more detail you add and the more will power you attach to your visualization of the future, the more limited the results will be. Usually, the greater the detail you project, the longer it takes to locate a resonant opportunity because there are far fewer of them. The more will power you generate to locate your goal opportunity, the more likely you are to plow under the best interests of other beings in search of their heart's desire. The focus of will power also creates a mind frame in which it is easy to overlook the fact that your opportunity has arrived. That is because will power is a critical faculty that creates more distinctions and reduces satisfaction with situations that don't match precisely the projection of goals. Said another way, details and will power add an edge and heaviness to your ritual request delaying the fulfillment of your goals on higher, lighter and purer levels the universe might otherwise offer.

By contrast, there are rituals based on emptiness. In these rituals, through relaxed awareness, you can forget yourself. In requesting the universe to resonate to your goals in this mind state, you place the least amount of conditions on the outcome. From this alone, there are more ways available to work out a satisfying fulfillment of your goals. So, what you do want can manifest more quickly. In the emptiness state of being, you connect with higher and subtler realms. The particular life problems or limitations your goals are directed toward, resolve themselves in more holistic and integrative ways because they originate from regions in the universe where everything is more intimately connected. Performing rituals with emptiness means accomplishing things without the complication or suffering of your ego. It is based on an intimate trust and connection with the higher places of the universe that although you can't sense, you can experience as the ground of all being.

CHAPTER 6

Meeting at the Right Place

Background as Foreground

In the process of buying and selling buildings, each of the places you go as an agent or buyer is like making an entrance on a stage production set. You may not be on a set for very long, but it could have an effect on the final outcome, depending on the actors present and if you have reached a critical scene. Part of the success of connecting sellers to buyers is managing the interactions. Some of that success is intuition. Some of the success is keen social awareness. Some of the success is learned salesmanship. This chapter will discuss enhancing your success by managing place (所) as a part of your discussions with sellers, buyers and all the people who come in between.

A realty sale is like a series of debates carried on in the emotional, logical, social, technical and financial arenas. It's a debate because there are a series of forced choices about location, building size, amenities, price, financing, lenders, and on and on. At every juncture, a new choice emerges out of the pros and cons possible. Each debate has a different set of rules and different decision makers. The energy of the physical places where these debates occur influence the decisions as much as the information and persuasion brought to bear there. Just as a football game or a battle, which is a clash of sides, is influenced by the arena, landscape and season, so too are realty sales. Learn to regard the background for these debates as more important to the outcome. Move the background to the foreground, and use it to your advantage.

Ichi Go Ichi E means "One moment, one meeting." In Japan, it is an adage associated with the tea ceremony, pointing out the uniqueness of each meeting with others. There is a mystical play of moment, people, purpose and place (所) that will never meet again.

Meeting Yin and Yang

If you are simply exchanging bits of information to fill in the shape of previous discussions this is ordinary conversation. The moment any information shared seems like it will influence a decision, however, communication, meetings and meeting places become important in moving forward. When you do need to meet in person, you may not have much of a choice as to whether you meet at an office, the client's home, or a restaurant because of scheduling. Yet, at your meeting site, there are a number of better or worse places depending upon your meeting's purpose. Meeting purposes correspond to the categories of yang and yin. Yang type meetings include creativity, brain-storming sessions, initial organizational meetings, check-up and follow-up meetings and formality appearances (legal or social). Yin type meetings include relationship building or repair, team building, consideration of details, and socializing. A good yin meeting results in a warm connection with all parties involved and shared consensus. A good yang meeting results in new ideas or decisions. A bad yin meeting stalls in emotional entanglements ending without direction. A bad yang meeting ends in power positions pushed down participants' throats despite valid concerns voiced about direction.

Neither yang nor yin is good by itself because life fluctuates between these two opposites. As moments change, yin or yang predominates, only later to switch to the opposite. Like a pendulum, life moves from yang to yin and back, over and over again. When you regard qualities of rooms, they can be grouped as yin or yang. A yang room has high ceilings, tile floors, many and tall windows, bright lighting, loud sounds, wide corridors, and space for crowds. A yin room has low ceilings, plush carpeting, a few windows, subdued or dark areas, muted sounds, narrow hallways, and space for a limited number of people, usually eight or less. Yang is best during daylight hours, resonates to circular shapes, is cool in temperature and is white or lighter in color. Yin is best during the evening and night hours, resonates to square or rectangular shapes, is warm in temperature and is dark in color. Look to match yang purposes with rooms that have yang qualities, and yin purposes with yin room qualities.

Yang Meetings

If you are generating creative ideas, speeding up negotiations, having an update meeting, or, desiring a definitive decision after preliminary discussions, you should seek spaces with yang qualities. That means find a large room with a circular table, lots of light, and that has more chairs than meeting participants. If the room is an interior room, turn up the lights to maximum and increase the air-conditioning to make it cooler. Leave the door open so that the hubbub of people passing by shifts the attention of meeting participants frequently. Serve iced or cold drinks.

Stand up a few times during the meeting to keep your energy moving. Encourage an atmosphere in which others can get up and move about. Invite a person to attend part of the meeting who is new to the process or group at large but has a new angle to contribute. If music is playing in the background, it should be lively, but not disruptive. Morning time is the best yang time, but any daylight hours will do.

Very typical yang spaces would be an outdoor café with ample street traffic during daytime, and non-meal time hours. A fast food establishment is the most yang among restaurants. Any public space, such as a comfortable park would do. Wherever population density is high, like a downtown area, there is much yang energy afoot. Indoors, a hotel lobby, convention center, or regional shopping mall are usually very yang places. At the office, a Board of Directors room that has more formality and large capacity is another yang space. Any large meeting room with a wall of windows, marble floors and is near the company reception area is a yang area. If you meet at a home, the living room, kitchen, or outdoor ramada or deck are the more yang locations. If you are meeting while driving around, it is an already yang environment made more yang in vehicles with larger interior spaces, like buses, vans, Rolls Royces, and stretch limousines.

Yin Meetings

If you are creating intimacy, slowing negotiations down, postponing decisions, or reviewing a number of detailed issues, then seek meeting spaces with a preponderance of yin qualities. That means find a smaller, interior room with a square or rectangular table, subdued lighting that can be dimmed, and that has just enough chairs for participants. In fact, if you have to add a chair so the room is cozy but not cramped, that is a good size room. Close the room door so that you diminish distractions. If you can't locate an interior, windowless room, then arrange the blinds or curtains so that light enters, but also so that meeting participants cannot see the coming and going of others. Serve hot coffee or teas or warm food. If it's a long meeting, take one break where everyone recesses and returns to the table at the same time. If a guest attends, it is best that it be someone all participants know, and who is good at facilitating group processes and relationship building. If background music plays, it should be calming, like classical music, but not be overly heavy or slow. Evening time from sunset to midnight are yin hours. Yin time extends till dawn, but the early morning hours are personal not public.

Very typical yin spaces would be dimly lit, out of the way restaurants during meal time hours. Any dining club or resort that prolongs the dining experience is a good yin setting. Wherever population density is low, like an out of the way spot overlooking a garden, river, lake or ocean, is a yin space. In a hotel, it would be a small meeting room or a suite with comforts and amenities at hand. Any place that encourages casual dress or behavior sets a yin tone. At an office, a yin meeting room is carpeted, has soft lighting, is informal, and comfortable. Such a room allows a peek into the personal lives of employees. It is usually a good place to darken the lights to make multimedia presentations. If you meet at a home, the dining room or a comfortable den are yin spaces most suitable for meetings. The most yin rooms in a home, the bathroom and bedroom are clearly not suitable for business. If there is a very small, walled, protected garden area, that outside space is a good yin place to meet. Usually cars are not good yin meeting places. If you have no choice though, a one-on-one meeting as you and your client sit in the front seat is the most yin arrangement possible in an auto. In general, any place that encourages personal connection or intimacy is a suitable yin space.

Eating and Meeting

In general, whenever you share a meal in the midst of realty arrangements, the connection becomes more personal. This is very important for realty agents who specialize in home sales. For commercial agents, a shared meal meeting is more effective when it's time to focus on options, or to close a deal. Meal meetings for commercial agents should become more frequent after the commitment decision to lease or buy through the time of signing the contract. For residential agents, establishing a relationship with viable buyers is important from the outset. That is because residential sales are yin realty while commercial leasing and sales are yang realty.

Meals are best taken in common with clients when a yin meeting is in order, when it is time to sift, focus, connect or celebrate. Yin meetings deteriorate when people become overly comfortable so that they concentrate on their own, subjective pleasures and views to the exclusion of outside business. A deteriorated yin meeting will postpone things to an indefinite future, or at worst mire down the whole process. Meals in common with clients should be avoided when strong, negative emotions are in play. That is because food, especially cooked food, has the ability to absorb emotions, energy, and consciousness. Drinking alcohol, rather than absorbing energy, opens a person's subconscious to emotions while losing the ability to selectively block negative ones. For instance, if there are many sharp and angry exchanges at a meal, the food will absorb that anger. Later when that food hits your digestive tract and blood stream, it brings anger inside. It makes it more difficult to let go of negative words and acts if you have eaten with people and digested their afflictive states. If you hadn't expected negativity when you sat down to a meal, but now find negativity unleashed, then limit your intake to non-alcoholic drinks or raw food, like salads.

The final caveat on meals is that in yang meeting situations, of updates, brainstorming, initial organization and decision-making, meals can hurt the process. The act of slowing down to share food subtracts from sharp, quick, creative, and decisive resolve that is the bedrock of yang meetings. So, in a yang meeting, it is fine to offer drinks, or even buffet style cold snacks where people help themselves. Remember not to waste the timely dispatch of agenda items with food focus. At times, you will work for clients that you dislike. In dealing with them during the entire process, meet outside of restaurants and cafes as it will limit your own dissatisfaction. Meals mixed with meetings, like everything else, have their positive and negative applications. Dine wisely.

Personalities, Meeting and Seating

People, like meetings and rooms, are divisible into yang and yin. In general, the strategy is to tone down excesses in either direction as long as you remember that excessive situations can be balanced by opposite types of excessive personalities, but not often. A yang personality is extroverted. Someone who is always talking, fidgeting, pacing, and doodling is a yang type person. They have short attention spans, and as a result keep changing the topic. They crave new stimulation. By contrast, yin personalities are introverted. Someone who thinks a lot, keeps quiet, and is somewhat shy are characteristics of a yin personality. Yin mindsets can stay focused on a single topic for a longer time. They can obsess over details, while the yang personality simply glosses across details.

Various life stages are ruled by yang and yin. Usually, children embody the most yang life stage. They run from distraction to distraction playfully. Seniors are at the most yin life stage. They sit for a long time watching, remembering, savoring, and appreciating. There are exceptions everywhere because you can always find a very quiet, in-turned child, or a non-stop, gabby octogenarian. Additionally, men are more yang in body type, while women are more yin. Again, you can find exceptions in the strong silent type man, or by contrast, in the over-the-top comedienne. From a practical point of view, judge whether the people involved in acquiring real estate are yang or yin by their personalities, then maintain dynamic balance.

As the conductor of the sales process, you know what can threaten or enhance the process. You also will come to know how the needs, goals, and personalities of your clients can subvert or further the process. As a last consideration of meetings, regard how seating order effects the meeting process and its outcome. Whether a room or meeting is yin or yang, various seating positions relative to doors, windows, and table shape have an independent effect on the proceedings. Next, we consider ways to judge whether the meeting effect is strong or weak.

Wealth Corner

Every room has a high focus location called the wealth corner. Different schools of feng shui place the wealth corner at different locations, for instance one view identifies the wealth position as southeast corner of a room. We locate the wealth corner by qi or energy flow created by the entry and room shape. As you walk into a room, you project your energy field ahead of you. From the door jamb, your energy and sightline are stopped by the opposite wall, then move toward the open area of the room which could be to the right or left. At the opposite diagonal, your energy passes through the far corner to return to you. The area corner is where the energy converges and collects and is the wealth corner. See Wealth Corner Image 11 on page 140.

There are three patterns. The room can open to the right, or to the left. In unusual cases, the door can open exactly in the middle of the room. In that case, there is a choice of which is the wealth corner. By drawing attention away from one side, and emphasizing the other corner by interior design the owner chooses the position of the wealth corner. The two walls moving toward the wealth corner have entering energy, while the other two walls have exiting energy. The middle walls are the more stable, while the extreme walls are places more open to change. Wealth corners are strongest where plain wall meets plain wall at the corner. Wealth corners are weakened when a door or window is located within six or less feet of the corner.

Wealth corners focus the room's energy. When symbols are placed there, the symbol moves more quickly from a representation, whether conscious or unconscious, to reality. We will return to the importance of this when we discuss staging in Chapter 8. Applied to meetings, the chairperson of the meeting should sit in one of the two wealth corner positions. The table shape will determine which seat has command of the room. If the table is square or perfectly round, then either place is a commanding place. If the table is rectangular or oval, the narrow portion of the table at the wealth corner has the commanding place. In most cases, the agent needs to manage the process and meetings, and so should take the commanding spot at a meeting. This is not easy to do if you meet at the home of the client as they may invoke home court advantage.

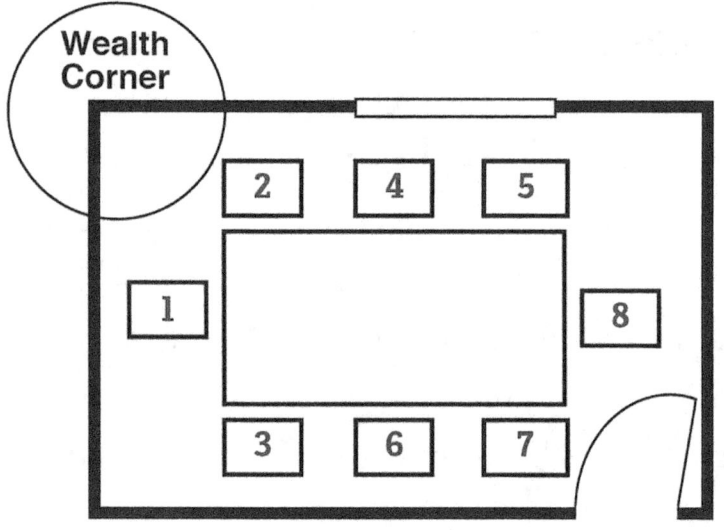

Meeting Room Seating: There are many room, table and seating combinations. When conducting meetings consciously using a feng shui approach, recognize which seats offer advantage or disadvantage to each participant. Sitting in the doorway is worst, but sitting back to the door is also a disadvantage, just not as severe. Windows, whether to the outside or to an inner corridor, distracts meeting participants.

All Chairs are not Equal

When you enter any room that could serve as a meeting room, survey the layout. The arrangement of chairs will reveal that certain places are stronger, neutral, or weaker. What increases the strength of a place positively is its relation to the wealth corner. What weakens a place is negative relation to doors and windows. There are a number of room layouts presented in the next few pages which compare the strength of position. We are expressing the strength of a position as numbers: -3, -2, -1, 0, +1, +2, +3. The negative numbers show weakening; neutral numbers show no effect; while positive numbers show strengthening.

There are other factors that also weaken or strengthen a position. Below is a table that lists them by number strength. The situations listed, unless otherwise indicated, refer to a room condition or item right behind the chair of a meeting participant.

Table 2: Meeting Position Modifiers

Number	Meeting room situations that modify position strength
-3	Open door to well-traveled hall, wet bar with alcoholic drinks available, fatal weapons that have been used to kill
-2	Mirror, closed door, magnificent view window, coffee bar or buffet, undersized chair, large artwork with disturbing images, being cramped up to wall, large meteorite, shamanistic or ritually active art, weapons, art and objects from churches, photos of animals hunting prey, seat under very loud or active HVAC vent, HVAC room unit, seat in front of a loud audio speaker
-1	Window, mildly irksome artwork, knife leaved plant or cactus, uncomfortable chair, mildly distracting wall color, phone, office equipment, large open space behind, small meteorite, pictures of weapons, seat under a noticeable HVAC vent
0	Blank wall in a neutral color
+1	Medium sized plant with rounded leaves, beautiful or protective art images that don't demand attention, harmonious nature photography, comfortable chair, ample space
+2	Proportionate, understandable wealth corner symbol, large size plant with rounded leaves, striking flower arrangement, proportionate geode, mineral or crystal, table-top fountain
+3	Ceiling is higher above this position, clerestory or high stained glass window above this position, chair is on a dais or raised above others, chair is larger and better appointed than others in room

Decision Influencers

Consider how important each person in attendance at any meeting is to influencing the decision at hand. You can rate each one on a scale like our others: -3, -2, -1, 0, +1, +2, +3. What you are rating is not whether a person is for or against the proposal you are recommending, but their weight in influencing the decision outcome. Next, predict whether you expect each person to be for or against the recommendations to be discussed at the meeting.

What will be the final outcome of these combined considerations? You can make an approximate estimation by drawing up an analysis table. Below we've included fictitious participants for a decision on whether to place (and perhaps how much) an offer on a 5,000-square foot, $3,900,000 estate home on a big-name golf course. Zed and Elaine (his fiancé) want to buy this place, but Zed's parents don't want him to buy a house that's 500 miles from their home. Fill in the table with the numbers that you determined from the decision influencer, position strength from the examples, and from the room modifiers table. Remember, if two or three room modifiers effect one person, add them all up to get just one room modifier number as below:

Table 3: Golf Course Property Offer

	Zed	Elaine	Mom	Dad
Decision Influencer	+3	-1	+2	+1
Position Strength	+1	+1	+2	-1
Room Modifiers	0	+2	+2	-2
TOTAL	+4	+2	+6	-2

Since Zed and Elaine are pro, their combined score is +6 as versus Mom and Dad whose combined score is +4 against the purchase.

Since Zed and Elaine's combined scores are greater than Mom and Dad's, Zed will probably make the offer. You can see it's close though. So, if you're managing this meeting with parents present, if you give Zed a better seat than his mom you will increase Zed's score significantly, and the overall probability that the meeting will move in the direction you recommend. To be in charge of this process, however, you will have to select the meeting place and scout it out beforehand so you know who should sit where. You can silence a too loud, uninformed voice by seating that person purposely in a bad place. You can also encourage a quiet, but good thinker to speak out more by offering that person a much better meeting chair location. You can also make sure that you do not take an inferior seat in the room when you have an important meeting to conduct.

We have explored being in the right place (所), especially during a meeting. Next chapter, we explore the contour of time, so you can assure that you are not only at the right place (所) but present at the right time.

CHAPTER 7

Meeting at the Right Time

The Law of Correspondence

When we look at the world, we see trillions upon trillions of phenomena. The ancient Chinese philosophers called it the "ten thousand things." Chemistry has reduced the complexity to 118 elements, while physics reduces it further to 17 subatomic particles. To work with the world, we have to simplify it; but, as we look, we find that simple patterns already exist. Managing our lives well means using simplicity to leverage complexity. Feng shui is a simplicity leverage system based using place (所) as the fulcrum. Cosmological feng shui uses astrology as a simplicity leverage system using the flow of time as the fulcrum. The cosmological school of feng shui reminds us that place (所) exists in coordinates of latitude and longitude, but also within a matrix of time. It draws our attention to the most obvious but often forgotten fact, that everything changes over time. Cosmological feng shui asserts that time is not just a background of life, but is a participating energy actively changing life events. This brings us to consider the astrological perspectives of time management.

Feng shui and astrology both work on the principle of correspondence. In simplifying the world to yin and yang, 5 agents, 7 pole stars, 8 I Ching *guas*, 9 flying stars, 10 planets, 12 zodiac constellations or any other division, we recognize that things group into patterns. Everything in that group vibrates at a similar frequency. They form a family of resonance. One member of the family corresponds to all the other members. When one member of the family changes, every member with resonating energy also changes to a greater or lesser degree. In feng shui for instance, you may want to change the energies influencing your career. After doing all you can directly, you may find yourself still well short of your career goals. By altering some smaller, more controllable and corresponding career resonating energy, you unleash change in your career. In astrology, each planet's position, motion, speed, and interrelation has been observed over millennia in order to determine how it resonates to a particular energy and how it corresponds to a set of similarities. When sky, star and planetary energies shift, it causes a corresponding shift in earth energy, and in life. Next follows a brief, but practical guide so you can navigate through the corresponding energies unleashed by time's flow.

All Times to Meet Are Not Equal

If you know in advance that a proposed meeting is merely informational, you don't need to analyze possible decision outcomes by player. The moment you meet, however, is also influenced by the pattern of all the stars, planets, meteors, galaxies and constellations relative to the horizons, the zenith and nadir. Although the cosmologic and astrologic considerations are complex, here are a few simple rules you can track and affirm by your own experience. What we will consider are moon cycles, eclipses, and the period of all the planets' retrograde motion.

The character for **Ming** is a fusion of sun on the left and moon on the right side. Together, these lights of the sky create daily and monthly cycles and literal brilliance. The *ming* symbol also refers to personal brilliance and profundity.

Regard the Moon

The closest heavenly body to the earth is the moon. Although it seems the moon merely orbits the earth, actually the earth and moon dance in a binary spiral around each other as they speed around the sun and the sun streaks around the galaxy. Each influences the other to a remarkable degree. The Chaldean and Babylonian magi fashioned an entire astrology based only on the moon cycles and zodiac location because they thought it the most important influence on earth life. Many cultures, including the Chinese, use the lunar mansions and a lunar calendar to measure the passage of time. All this means that from ancient times and across the entire earth, people from many cultures noted the consistent and important effects that moon motions have on human behavior.

The most regular and obvious astronomical event to notice is the moon cycle, especially the new and full moons that happen about every two weeks. What new or full moons do is focus greater energy into any moment in which events, ideas, emotions and actions have been considered, but held back. At the new or full moon days, energies and events that have been massing tend to pour more freely into the world. Usually consider the peak range of influence of the new and full moons to be the day plus or minus two more days. Meetings conducted at these times tend to be more significant than we might otherwise expect.

When lunar or solar eclipses occur, the strength of the full and new moons effectively triples. It is very easy to miscalculate the undercurrents in any realty purchase process at these times. Most calendars show when new and full moons occur. Appendix 1 lists when solar and lunar eclipses occur from 2015 to 2050. Be cautious at least 5 days before or after any eclipse. The most powerfully influential eclipse on a local area is unleashed by a total solar eclipse where the path of totality creates a lunar shadow over the place that you live. The next one in North America will be on **August 21, 2017**. It is very easy to use the internet to explore any solar eclipse shadow paths, often providing you more scientific data than you will need to conduct a great realty meeting. On the internet, you easily can find the August 21, 2017 shadow path.

Planet Station Point and Retrograde Periods

Owing to the varying speeds and elliptical orbits of earth and the other planets, there are times each year when it appears that a planet reverses itself and moves backwards. Of course, no planet moves backwards, and that fact would be obvious were we observing from the 6,000ºC surface of the sun. From the temperate earth view, all the planets at some time or other in their orbits appear to move backwards. That motion is called retrograde. From earth, only the sun and moon never retrograde. All the other planets do. When each planet switches the apparent direction of its motion from direct to retrograde or back from retrograde to direct, it seems that the planet is suspended, almost unmoving in space.

During these standstill periods, some aspects of a business deal or personal situation become more intense and hence more unstable. These periods last from two days to two weeks. There are eight planets that switch directions back and forward about once a year, except for Mercury, which does it three to four times annually. That means altogether there are about 26 to 30 periods to watch. Adding new and full moons to this, there are about 50 periods to watch, or there is about one wrinkle in time each week on average. During some weeks, however, two or more events overlap to produce particularly memorable and accelerated moments and transactions.

What follows is a discussion of the eight planets during their most intense periods, the time of apparent standstill. Although many entire books have been published about the effects of this phenomenon, we are limiting consideration to two aspects particularly important to real estate sales. The first has to do with how the purchase or escrow process might shift during standstills.

The second has to do with what realty issues may move to the forefront to become a focal consideration. We also are including a bit of advice on how to mitigate difficulties that may arise. During these times, seeing things in balanced context becomes challenging for buyers, sellers and realty agents because side issues get distorted out of context and out of proportion. The standstill planets can alert you as to which side issues are likely to monopolize the analysis and drive the process. Appendix 2 lists the times of the eight planets' retrograde and standstill periods so you will know when to take the right balancing actions.

Mercury Standstills and Retrograde Periods

Process: Mercury's motion is important to watch in business and communication of all kinds. When Mercury retrogrades, it lasts about nineteen to twenty -three days each occurrence before returning to forward motion. You need to watch the whole retrograde period for Mercury and be especially cautious if contract deadlines fall a day or two on either side of the actual standstill day. Because there are three to four retrograde episodes annually, there are two to three months each year when temporarily dysfunctional Mercury, messenger of the gods, brings challenges to your business and personal life. Each of the visible planets functions more prominently on a particular weekday, and Mercury's best day is Wednesday.

Retrograde Mercury's most likely business process dysfunctions are that errors inadvertently get written into documents. This includes contracts, ads, business cards, signs, and presentations. Usually the cause is misspelling, inverted numbers, or miscopied data due to hasty editing. In conversation, misinformation is spoken, heard or learned. Legal papers take longer to process because of a riot of little mistakes: i's not dotted, t's not crossed, signatories hard to find. More steps or negotiations are added to any process, usually in response to the situation at hand. Government, regulatory and financial bodies, and their staff, hold you to fulfilling the letter of the law. It's usually on account of the bureaucratic system and is not personal. It takes three to five times the amount of phone calls, letters, memos or conversations to unearth a piece of data you're looking for. Phone, computer and communications equipment failure may compound these tasks. So, may courier, postal and delivery service errors. You spend many more hours and miles in your car commuting to various places in efforts to connect with the right people with the right information.

Place and Property: Mercury retrograde place issues are about mail delivery and mail boxes. They involve traffic flow on foot, on bike and by car as well as public transportation considerations. They also involve commuting patterns and ease of routes. They involve the presence of elementary, middle or high schools in the neighborhood and the educational rating of school districts. They involve the community that surrounds a house or business. It may involve the name recognition of the neighborhood, it's social problems or traffic issues. Are there community gardens and indications of active or passive social interactions in the community? The proximity or distance to health care facilities or providers may also become a key issue.

Countermeasures: None of the above outcomes are life-threatening and the period involved is tolerably about three weeks long. In fact, most Mercury retrograde outcomes are often annoying details that result in redoing things at some extra expense. The first countermeasure is to plan that the process will take more time so you can attend to the details as they arise. Don't promise expeditious outcomes; rather, promise due diligence. The second countermeasure is to take your time to check, double and triple recheck anything on paper, in print, on slides, or on the web. Do this whether you generated the document or are reviewing it. The third countermeasure is to listen carefully to conversations, and verbally recap information you learned to see if you recorded it correctly in your memory. The final countermeasure is don't let details slide. This is the time when lack of attention to fine print and diligent process will receive negative notice from your suppliers, sub-contractors, employees, colleagues, and clients.

Venus Standstills

Venus changes direction about once every nineteen months and operates in retrograde motion for forty-two days. When Venus changes direction be careful that day and one day on either side.

Fortunately, it's influence as a retrograde planet is much less frequent than the other planets, excepting Mars, which has the least frequent retrograde cycle of all. Venus as the goddess Aphrodite symbolizes all things beautiful, artful, easy and comfortable, yet expensive. The influence of Venus functions best on Friday.

Process: The main Venus process issues revolve around money: prices, budgets, affordability, loans, rates, all cash transactions, payment for third party inspections, who pays for repairs, and who doesn't. In terms of interactions, there is a premium on manners, civility and social harmony in negotiations and in meetings. Often, buyers and sellers may already know one another or be connected by social ties, like being members of the same church, business or social organization. They may hail from the same area of the country, the same university, or same career field. During the Venus standstill, previous social connections influence the process, usually in positive directions.

Place and Property: When it comes to the actual property, social and aesthetic characteristics become emphasized. For instance, curb appeal, the look of a well-appointed neighborhood, tasteful landscaping, and congenial neighbors seem like more important considerations. Whether the neighborhood has beautiful parks or a variety of unique restaurants and genteel businesses increases the perceived value for the potential buyer. The home or building layout, it's color scheme, it's proportion, and overall beauty and comfort move to the forefront of criteria and motivation for purchase.

Countermeasures: Don't gloss over a client's concerns about how things look. For instance, their perception of a wall color as odd merits suggesting easy alternatives. Encourage prospective buyers to talk to neighbors especially during these periods. In terms of meeting and searches, clients appreciate more care as the process unfolds, providing them with comfortable and beautiful spaces in which to rest and talk, and from which to appreciate the social and aesthetic comforts that could well ease their everyday routines. Stopping for meals, snacks or creature comfort needs at more upscale locations creates a stronger social bond with buyers. That social, rather than business, connection in turn increases client confidence in your professional ability to help them obtain their desired lifestyle rather than a bare property. You are acting as a member of a community who can connect them skillfully to that community.

Mars Standstills

The planet, Mars, exhibits retrograde motion about every 25 months, but its change of motion periods occur over a three or four-day course. The total time Mars moves in arrears is about eighty days. Even though the two Mars standstill periods happen just two percent of any year, the infrequent occurrence is nonetheless filled with volatility and verve. Mars, which resonates best on Tuesday, has a strong association with warfare and pushes that influence to the forefront.

Process: All parties to the realty transaction seem easily irritated or are downright angry and aggressive in their demeanor. Everybody wants the process to move faster and faster with buyers or sellers often becoming incensed when delays arise. This period is characterized by hardball negotiations, risks, angry exchanges, direct, no nonsense attitudes and the pressure to take shortcuts to accelerate the deal. The tone of the process reflects rivalry over cooperation and win-lose thinking rather than win-win. It can be predatory at its lowest moments. It can be your quickest and most skillfully expeditious transaction at its highest moments.

Place and Property: The issues raised during the Mars standstill involve the neighborhood presence or absence of fire stations, police stations, crime, martial arts dojos, fitness gyms, sports venues, playing fields, or of outdoor sports or gun stores. Other neighborhood considerations are barking dogs, hostile neighbors, proximity of major streets, speeding traffic, bright night lights, or frequent smoke and smells. Building issues can be about non-permitted improvements or unskilled or substandard repairs, broken fixtures, fireplaces, or badly worn floors, walls or foundations.

Countermeasures: Keep a clear head and stay as calm and patient as you can to diffuse the aggression, irritation and impatience of others. You will probably have to work faster and harder to keep up the pace. This is not the moment to relax and chat with clients as they don't value creature comforts. They want progress, resolution and action instead. They value your speed and skill and demand straight talk. Plan to get up earlier and work later.

Jupiter Standstills

Jupiter, and all the planets beyond it, change direction and create standstill periods twice a year. Jupiter standstill periods occur over a five-day period on average, and it remains in retrograde motion for about four months a year. Jupiter is the largest planet, the king of the gods, always in grand appearance, full of pomp and circumstance. Jupiter is associated with Thursday.

Process: With Jupiter standstills, the process can become political whether it be family or city politics. Outside influencers become more central at every stage of the sale and escrow, and their influence may last well beyond closing. Contract law and legal requirements of zoning, easements, building code, or HOA restrictions become emphasized issues as the transaction unfolds. Contractor or homeowner obtained building permits or certificates of occupancy become decision hinges. The period of buyer due diligence becomes crucial as does every other legal step of the contract execution.

Place and Property: Big neighborhood issues during the Jupiter standstill are about status, the proximity of cultural amenities, country clubs, upscale businesses, high end retail, universities, museums, dance and opera venues, major sports arenas, churches, and gentrified areas. Political boundaries, like city or county jurisdiction color property choices. Home or any other building issues revolve around high culture, grand appearance, wealth, privilege or exclusivity.

Countermeasures: Pay close attention to executing the realty contract as written. Call in experts early to give precise advice about gray area issues. Don't get lazy. Don't assume anything. Protect your client's rights closely. Take every opportunity to showcase amenities of the house or area. If your clients are world citizens, they need to appreciate how international and sophisticated an enclave or house actually is. Finally, you may need to enlist an ally with political clout to help resolve issues that are meeting with unreasonable bureaucratic resistance.

Saturn Standstills

The planet Saturn, associated with Saturday, mercifully only changes direction twice a year, once backing up, and once returning to forward motion. Saturn is associated with the earth and is the slowest moving of the planets visible to the naked eye. Saturn is associated with the god, Kronos, or time itself. Saturn standstills require paying attention to two types of time considerations. The first is the period that is five days on either side of the Saturn standstill day. The second period is the entire period of backward motion lasting about 140 days. The longer period is applicable to longer term projects such as zoning or planning permits, or to remodeling. Usually, problems which first arose under the Saturn standstill days don't develop enough momentum to become solvable until Saturn moves into a direct motion again.

Process: There are unforeseen and long delays. Progress slows to a crawl. If things were going very slowly before, then this period might end the enterprise in fatal entropy. Legal and contractual deadlines cause problems. Governmental bodies, agencies and their representatives push their authority, usually imposing additional requirements. People in bureaucratic authority table decisions to a later time. Often, there are delays in getting additional financing packages together. Real estate agents host more protracted excursions in search of the right property. You or your clients may become physically exhausted because you've stretched yourselves beyond habitually healthy living and work patterns. To obtain, construct or remodel property, or to comply with planning and building codes requires much more investment than originally estimated. Finally, meetings may get postponed or cancelled because participants are overloaded with work or work schedules.

Place and Property: During Saturn standstills, concerns are likely to arise over practical real estate matters: boundary definitions, property access, soils conditions, mineral rights, mold, building structure, excavations; buried utilities, public archaeological interests, building plan compliance, zoning compliance, earthquake fault zones, building foundations, stone and cement patios, sidewalks and driveways, brick or earthen structures, environmental or industrial degradation of land and buildings, and, legal condemnation of decaying property Clients may seriously consider run-down, moldy, dirty, noisy or otherwise austere neighborhoods and properties. Fixer-upper properties receive more detailed consideration.

Countermeasures: Saturn standstill periods all boil down to developing and practicing infinite patience under trying circumstances. Specifically, defiant opposition to government or its representatives leads to defeat because you and the client do not have the weight or resources to countermand what can be pitted against you. Therefore, negotiate with regulators, don't demand concessions. Another countermeasure is to budget extra time, especially if you expect a property to close during the Saturn standstill. Because there is a lot that demands your attention, be careful not to exhaust yourself. Calm, patient and measured actions are the best responses to the Saturn standstill events. Once you've watched what happens in a cycle or two, you will know how to apply caution, shrewd assessment, and stamina to succeed during the Saturn standstill periods.

Uranus Standstills

The three outer planets cannot be seen without binoculars or telescope and do not influence the days of the week. They are so far away from earth and they each bring an impersonal cast to earthly events. Uranus is associated with the ancient god of the sky and the original order of the heavens. Uranus is associated with freedom and fairness and was discovered in 1781, the year the U.S. Constitution was signed. Uranus also is associated with sudden events, science and radical change. Uranus will change direction backward then forward each year and remain in retrograde for about 155 days. The Uranus standstill period lasts for about five days.

Process: Sudden and out of the blue changes happen. Parties to the contract may take some unilateral or rebellious action. Information that is provided by electronics, computers, or websites may contain glitches or inaccurate data. Electronic processing, which most real estate transactions use, may become garbled, or temporarily inaccessible.

Place and Property: Neighborhood issues are about airports and air traffic, Air Force bases, reliability and speed of internet, TV, and cell phone coverage. Other concerns are about start-up or techie businesses nearby, how avant-garde an area is becoming, or how many new and innovative buildings are being constructed in the neighborhood. Questions about the electrical power and wiring of buildings as well as solar power and other innovative tech upgrades to buildings become important. Integrated computer and entertainment systems with home theatres especially will motivate potential buyers.

Countermeasures: Don't make radical changes, but sufficient enough to resolve present concerns. Check and re-check your printouts and emails for accuracy. Back up all your documents – even redundantly. It is important to be fair and transparent during this period. Your tech-savvy clients will want all manner of data and information. Whatever info you can provide directly or can point them toward indirectly will create greater mutual trust as you resolve their questions and support their analytical process.

Neptune Standstills

Each year, the Neptune standstill period is five or six days while the complete retrograde period is about 160 days, or about five and a third months. As one of the elder gods with Uranus, Saturn, and Pluto, Neptune connects back to the past. Usually the slower planets require us to resolve a tangle of issues older than this contract, maybe even older than a particular building being bought or sold, or even a previous building zoning designation.

Process: During Neptune periods, thinking is unduly influenced by delusive assumptions. Betrayal, whether projected or actual, poisons relationships. Hidden obstacles from hidden obstructors deliberately placed in our paths need skillful removal. The severe obsessions or addictions of any of the parties, especially, around alcohol or drugs hinders the process. On a less difficult level, parties or their representatives, display episodes of irresponsible behavior, whether in conversations or around contract agreements or timelines.

Place and Property: At the neighborhood level, Neptune period concerns center on superfund areas that are or have been under significant environmental remediation. They also concern churches, hospitals, nursing homes, group homes, halfway houses or alleged drug trafficking in the area. The presence or absence of bars, dance clubs, live music venues, yoga studios, art districts, marinas, or water frontage becomes important to the buyers or sellers. For the building itself, issues about ghosts, lead based paint, asbestos, mold, leaking roofs or walls, flood prone areas, previous presence of meth labs or any other chemical impact to the building becomes a major concern.

Countermeasures: Don't entertain clients with alcohol and expect coherent analysis or action. You may need to provide fact check moments directly or indirectly. Don't try to hide or obscure details from any of the parties. Encourage buyers to be extra vigilant in their examination of the property and its surrounding area. Don't space out. Be clear and engage a positive attitude.

Pluto Standstills

Despite the demotion of Pluto by a vote of 424 of the world's 10,000 professional astronomers to dwarf planet status, don't underestimate the influence that the god of death and the underworld still wields. Pluto, as a far-out planet, retrogrades just once a year. It's total period of backward motion is around 165 days or about five and a half months. Whenever it appears to stand still, it's period can be from six to fourteen days owing to its eccentric orbit.

Process: Pluto standstill periods add intensity of feeling, volatility and consequence to whatever is happening. Larger scale concerns, and backroom meddling become injected into the process, at times imperiling successful completion of escrow. Unequal power relationships dominate dealings. Credit, mortgages, financing, taxes, and insurance become the control issues that must be satisfactorily resolved or else, no sale.

Place and Property: Neighborhood concerns are about probable crime activity, especially overall crime statistics, gang presence and location of convicted sex offenders. On the opposite side of the spectrum, gated communities, private security, and extremely exclusive and expensive properties are highlighted. As to the building, discovery of deliberate cover-ups of anything from repairs, to violations of zoning or other legal obligations bedevils not just trust, but the sale itself.

Countermeasures: Avoid heavy-handed pressure. Attend quickly to any hint that financing may not proceed on time or to final funding.

Avoid even the merest appearance of sexual harassment. Do not go into compromising or dangerous situations or places. Be particularly mindful of safety. It is never good realty agent policy to give tax, financing or accounting advice, but to do so during this period may expose you to actionable and negative consequences for giving that kind of advice. Unethical or illegal behavior, or its appearance, is more likely to become exposed, now or much later. Don't acquiesce to forced, secretive, or unseemly actions whether you are pressured by brokers, other agents or your own clients. Protect your reputation and your future.

Meeting Critical Index

The last consideration is how do the time periods we just discussed effect the process. Below is a table rating meetings from 1, low impact, to 5, critical impact. A second table lists a number value for the time periods we just discussed.

Table 4: Rating Meeting Criticality

Meeting Rating	Reasons for Meeting
1	Casual social connection outside work, no business agenda
2	Information exchange, updates, progress checks
3	Negotiations, instructions, making dependent decisions
4	Project threatening issues: can lose or gain specific business
5	Relationship threatening issues: can lose or gain a client

Table 5: Meeting Timing Multipliers

Meeting Multiplier	Reasons for Meeting
1.33	Mercury retrograde period (about three weeks)
1.50	Mercury or Venus standstill (date of change + or – one day)
1.60	Mars or Jupiter standstill (date of change + or – two days)
1.70	Saturn standstill (date of change + or – two days)
1.80	Uranus, Neptune or Pluto standstill (+ or – three days)
2.00	New or full moon
6.00	Lunar or solar eclipse
12.00	Total solar eclipse and your location is in the path of total shadow

Once you know the kind of meeting that you are planning to have, find its criticality rating in Table 4. If no modifying timing event is happening, then the meeting is as critical as you expect. If a modifying event as listed in Table 5 is happening, the meeting increases in criticality. To find out how much, multiply the meeting multiplier event number times the meeting rating number. For instance, a planned negotiation is (3), but, on a Mercury standstill (meeting multiplier = 1.5), multiply (3) times (1.5) to calculate a critical index of 4.5. Or an information exchange (2) is scheduled during a new moon (2) to make a critical index of 4. Even a simple social connection of (1) gets increased if it is scheduled during a Mercury retrograde (1.3) and lunar eclipse (6) yielding a (1 x 1.3 x 6) high rating of 7.8. In other words, the meeting is likely to hold more surprises than what you might expect. A last example is that if at a lunar eclipse there is also a Mercury standstill time, during which you hold a relationship critical meeting (5), the criticality of this meeting now jumps to 39 (5 x 1.3 x 6)! Your entire business life could be effected by great loss or great gain by this one meeting at that moment.

Moments of time can diminish or exaggerate interactions whether they be geological epochs, historical eras or personal peaks. When speaking of timing, there are many more events and distinctions we could draw, but the intent here is to stimulate your awareness by watching how a few timings effect your own business life's ebb and flow. As you see what occurs, you can apply countermeasures, including feng shui meeting management, to stabilize and improve your business meeting outcomes.

CHAPTER 8

Staging for Staging

We now consider what most people consider the core of real estate feng shui: what color, shape, and material changes can induce the look, feeling and behavior changes around a piece of property? What will make it sell tomorrow afternoon for 10% over the asking price? Or sooner and for more profit? The first strategy is to get realty shoppers to stop and see for themselves what is here. In a few seconds of a drive-by of several hundred feet at 30 to 50 miles per hour, the appearance of the house has to register very positively. The desired behavior change has to induce shoppers to slow down, turn around and stop. That means they are viewing and responding to the overall impression very quickly, almost subliminally. So, the property must supply them something swiftly upon which to focus their fleeting attentions.

There are three types of focal energy that will attract a passerby to stop. The first is compatible focus. That is not so much a focus as a pre-existing match between the overall energy pattern of the house and of a particular person passing by. No matter how focused or scattered the energy of the place, only persons with matching energy field signatures will find the property engaging. The second is a thorough focus which occurs when all the parts of the property cohere and work with each other to broadcast an attuned, strong and unitary energy field. When you're living or working in a place, you'll want to create thorough focus. When you're selling though, creating a thorough focus is not cost effective effort. So, in realty sales or leases, assure that the third type, a workable focus is in place. A workable focus is that at each step of the way (front yard, foyer, living room, etc.) a sufficient energy radiates at each step to induce a person to want to enter the next area. What you are creating is links between rooms rather than a consistent underlying pattern in all rooms and areas of the property.

Stringing Pearls Along a Cord of Awareness

The gospel of Matthew admonishes that we should not cast pearls before swine, and that is also good feng shui advice. Think of each specific place on a property, specifically individual rooms, alcoves, front yards, side yards, niches, pool areas and protected arbors, as various precious and semi-precious stones with the odd few rocks thrown in the mix. To create sufficient or working focus for a person to want to tour a property, there have to be enough connected energies that either push or pull the person along to the next step. If you want people to stroll through the property, you have to string the valuable places (pearls) together in a compelling enough way along the thread of their awareness. Tactically, no one place should be over-compelling, although you can easily disguise negative rooms with neutrality so they become forgotten, temporarily at least.

The Fast Focus on Connecting

The most common view of any property is from the car that is either cruising or careening past, and this is especially so as more of America's community neighborhoods become commuting residential areas. The easier and more appealing that the approach to any commercial or residential property appears, the more it will magnetize contacts including in-person, phone, email, and postal contacts. Oddly, this is even more valid the faster observers speed past a property. The front entrance and the path to get there are the essentials of the invitation to create a connection. It will be impossible to create a workable focus without the initial connection that lands the passerby mentally on the doorstep to later be lured in by other engaging features. For the moment, let's look at the components of creating that connection:

1. The landscape context
2. The path (or lack thereof) to the entry
3. The frame around the entry area
4. The target door

Landscape Context

The landscape in front of any building can serve to create a central focal area, or else to disperse the view among fragmented areas. Good front yard feng shui serves to point from several quarters squarely to the front door. It has to make an aesthetic, yet unambiguous statement. That means that the closer you get to the main entry, the more dramatic and intense the front landscaping should become in shape, color, and tone. Not enough and too much landscaping are just two ways to arrive at the same result: diminishing building appeal. With trees, bushes, fences, fountains, sculptures, signs and walkways, many things work only if they are proportional to the size of the building that they are intended to point out. In order to prepare the landscape context properly, do the following:

1. Trim away all the overgrowth of bushes, trees, grass and ground covers. This is especially important closest to the front door. The aim is to achieve an ample sense of entry space that easily can accommodate a group of simultaneous visitors.

2. Put flowers or plants in pots near the front door. The more brilliant foliage colors, especially red, should be closer to the door, while the subtler colors should fade away outwardly toward the edges.

3. Remove manmade landscape features, like rustic wagons, that are large, but near property borders. It is better if they are more proximate and point out the entry as long as they do not detract from the entry area visually or in terms of cramping space.

4. Landscape decorations should be consistent with or in a complementary style to the building environment: no flock of pink, plaster flamingos popping out of a St. Cloud, Minnesota snow drift for instance. Or no Northwest Coast Indian totem pole outside a two-story Tudor.

5. View the night lighting of the landscaping to check for coherent emphasis. The brightest lighting should be directed around and at the front entry, with walkways amply indicated. Up-lighting trees, or spot-lighting bushes at a distance from the front only makes sense if you are highlighting the boundaries of a property. In that way, the lights point out the property from its neighbors upon a distant approach.

6. The 2-car or 3-car driveway creates a mass of cement that unbalances landscaping visually and materially. De-emphasize the driveway area, and emphasize the entry area all the more. The larger the driveway is as a percentage of the front yard, the more dramatic the landscaping needs to be to point out the front door.

The Path to Enter and a Portal

How to get from the street to the front door of a house or office building is the question anyone approaching a place must ask. If no path is indicated, that presents a problem to the visitor who must blaze a trail in search of entry. If the entry is hard to see, the visitor may conclude there is no ready connection. To overcome that defect, the visitor has to have a strong motivation to want in. Most people, including potential customers, do not have barrier-breaking motivation. So, the inhabitant or the realty agent must eliminate the barrier and establish a connecting pathway. This is true even in the three cars per household lifestyle where most everyone drives and walking is just a form of cardiac exercise rather than local travel.

Consider the sidewalk to the entry door more as an enabling connector from the private worlds of business or home to the great world outside. This path is a neighborhood earth meridian as are streets and public sidewalks. The neighborhood property must activate its earth meridian connection to the larger grid of pathways of streets, avenues, highways, and walkways. Even if these are all man-made meridians, they nonetheless function to connect society. Having no walkway from a house to the street is like having no phone line, cable line, electric line, water line or sewage line to the larger world. No connecting link means no connection is likely via that media to the larger world. Walkways connect people to communities in a grounded way. So simple, so profound, yet so ignored in the last twenty years!

What are the guides for creating a good connecting pathway?

1. There should be a path independent of the driveway along which visitors can walk the entire distance from the street to the door.

2. The path must be proportional to the height of the house and the distance from the street to the front door. A mansion must have a wide and grand walk up to its doors, whereas a single-floor bungalow needs a walk width minimally sized so two people can walk comfortably side-by-side.

3. A very long distance from street to door requires a path that meanders in gentle curves. A long, straight walkway, though clear on where to connect, funnels an accelerated energy to the front

door that ultimately disrupts visitors by attracting them then dispersing them prematurely. Turns in the walkway angle should occur every seven to nine paces, or about every 21 to 27 feet.

4. A very long pathway can be improved by being made of flagstone, brick, or some surface other than untreated cement that shows some variation in line, shape and color along the way.

5. A long pathway should have nodes along the way, a larger paved square shape for instance should be part of a long walkway to regulate approaching energy into a comfortable flow for visitors and inhabitants. Pause areas should be staggered every fourteen to eighteen paces, or about every 42 to 54 feet.

6. Short paths less than three paces or nine feet, should be more like approach patios rather than sidewalks. The paving materials should have color and variation. The front approach should have the feel of an outdoor, open air foyer or lobby even if there is an inside one.

7. Pathways should be broader, whatever their average width, at the points of connection to the public sidewalk or street and at the other end, the entrance. The widening should be greater at the entrance.

Picture This

The doorway area may be a physical door that goes directly into the building, or it may be a gated door through a fence or foliage that obscures direct sight of the building. Whichever case, this area must become focal. When you consider a door itself, you are looking at a rectangle of 21 square feet. Even a large double door of eight feet may cover an opening of only 64 square feet in a square shape. Relative to the front area, this amount may represent less than 10 percent of the visible face of the entry side of the building. In many storied commercial or residential buildings, the doorway's percent size of the building face diminishes by half for every floor. To make the door bigger, you frame it in trees, bushes, sculpture, rocks, fountains or an open or covered entry patio. If these items work correctly, they will seem like extensions of the door. The framing materials will then seem to radiate outward and will make the entry a greater, easier, and more inviting destination.

To understand what you are framing, you have to stand across the street from any building and look on for a good while with the perspective of a movie director. In the first frames of scene one, you have to motivate the viewer to want to walk into the heart of your drama, comedy or action adventure. The front entry may project barrier or magnetic energy. From across the street looking on, you have enough perspective to discover whether the entry beckons, repels, scatters or hides the lives or business of the inhabitants. Your job is to ensure that the projected message of the entry is to beckon warmly as well as make access easy. The purpose of framing the entry is to give you more material and literally latitude with which to adjust the welcoming signal than merely the square footage of the front door. A frame directs perspective. It cuts off the unnecessary and highlights the essence. A good frame disappears so that you don't even notice there is one. That's the second objective in framing the door.

Doors with Magnetic Charm

Within the frame, the most important view is the door. No part of the landscaping should draw your attention away from the door. Whatever the colors of the house, the door should be a brighter shade of the trim color, or it should contain one more color not shown anywhere else on the building so that the door is a completely unique feature. Classical feng shui says the door should be red, metallic gold, or red and bronze. Red is the color of activation on this planet, so it is the most eye-catching color. It's not subtle, but it's very effective. Even if you only strategically highlight the door trim or a beam above the door in red, you will discover that passing a property at 45 miles per hour, a little red paint still jolts the awareness of a passerby. If you can't use red paint, add some red flowers, banners with red, or lighting that makes the doorway glow like an ember in the dark of night. If you don't use red at all, you can still succeed in magnetizing attention to the door, but you'll need some help from the orange yellow part of the light spectrum. Warm metal highlights as in gold, copper or bronze will also work to magnetize attention. The objective is to magnetize attention so well that a motive to view the property is established.

Staging the Near, the Far and the Attractive

A person lands upon the threshold and contemplates the front door for a few moments before it opens. When the door does open, an overall energy force is unleashed that will pull, repel or have no motive effect on the visitor. That force that seems like a single entity and can be apprehended in a single moment is an aggregate of the energies of the people living there, furniture, building materials, shapes, symbols, smells, orientation to the cardinal directions, to other buildings, and to the stars. It is also made up of every thought, word and action of everyone ever on the site. A certain thread ties it all together, the weak forces are masked by the stronger forces. When the thread is very coherent, you experience thorough feng shui that comes in good and bad varieties. When the thread connects to the next step, you experience workable feng shui, also in good and bad varieties. The art of staging a house or office is to decorate it with items at powerful arrangement points that create the workable feng shui energy thread needed to sell.

In staging for sales, whether you use the furniture and artworks of the occupants or rent accoutrements temporarily, there are three considerations to replicate room by room:

1. Creating entering focus

2. Centering wealth corner focus

3. Refining essential views

The character for **Men** looks like a gate. It means an entryway literally and more figuratively as a passage point into a new realm. It can also mean "*system*."

Enter Here!

As you approach a doorway near enough to enter a room, there should be some close-at-hand furniture piece, sculpture or artwork that draws your attention, and ultimately your first few footsteps into that room. There is a delicate balance to achieve. The piece that draws you forward cannot be so inspiring or exquisite that it stops all forward progress. Yet another purpose of that same piece is to set a tone, or announce a theme that the room will explicate in greater detail once you enter. If you were writing a novel, this literary technique would be foreshadowing. This theme piece, especially if it is an artwork, can be changed so that it matches the season or captures a fleeting moment of special celebration. Suggestions for entry artwork are pictures or photos with happy families (like the potential buyers, only happier), or warm, tender moments relative to the room (dining, conversing, cooking, jovial socializing, studying the world, etc.). The art should have a positive emotional tone without heavy or dark colors or moods. Landscapes in the foreground of entry should be comfortable and welcoming, but not spectacular. Furniture likewise should be welcoming, interesting, but not over the top.

The size of the entry art or furniture needs to be proportional to the display area and the size of the room. Any art or interior decoration viewed from twelve or more feet away has to be large enough to reveal some detail at that distance. At twelve feet away, an entry piece usually needs to be at least 3-foot-high by about 2 feet wide. That is a rough approximation, not an absolute rule. Always the piece has to seem right for a specific place in the room. Entry ensembles of art, furniture, decorations and plants can be set to beckon, but the number of items tied together in the entry tableau should be spare, not more than seven at most for a very large room. Three to five items are a better number for foyers, living rooms, dining rooms, hallways, family rooms, and some home offices. One is the most focused invitation possible. Usually, yang or odd numbers of items create action and match the function of yang rooms. Even or yin numbers of pieces create quieter, more stable atmospheres compatible with yin rooms such as bathrooms, bedrooms, dens, and sitting rooms.

Wealth Corners as Positive Messages

We discussed wealth corners and how to locate them in Chapter 6 and provide a diagram below. Wealth corners aggregate and focus energy sometimes quickly, sometimes slowly. Any wealth corner transforms the symbols placed there from being a static arrangement of art, decorations, tools, plants, and window and wall space into attracting action with verifiable results.

What should a wealth corner contain? It should feature two kinds of objects: symbols and nurturers. Symbols are photos, pictures, altars, shrines, decorations, sculptures, appliances, and tools. These are primary activators that display a goal in symbol form that will magnetize actions, accomplishments and regrets. Nurturers are plants, fountains, geodes, crystals, mineral laden rocks, lamps, lights, fireplaces, skylights, clerestory windows, translucent (but not clear) windows and colors. This latter class contains all manner of living energies. Being alive, nurturers add and draw life energy into the wealth corner so as to accelerate transforming the displayed symbol into palpable life change. Although not as powerful, nurturers, pictures, photos and other secondary representations of moving water, crystals, flora and fauna also help transform symbols into action. The wealth corner ensemble should be the most eye-catching and ultimate focus for the room.

What specifically should the wealth corner contain? Whatever your goal, a symbol expressing that very goal amid nurturing plants is a simple yet effective wealth corner arrangement. Plants and artwork must be arranged in proportion to the room size. Grand rooms require grand sizes. Cottages require intimacy. Since the goal is to sell the home or office, what symbols a realty agent places in the wealth corner are the agents' 3-dimensional understanding of the target market and its motivations. They are of a species of advertising image with which buyers can identify. The main marketing picture, a sales presentation in a glance, should be located in the living room. "Living room" here means the room where the owners and their friends actually gather for conversation and entertainment. Here is a list of compatible symbols that wealth corners in the other rooms should contain:

Table 6: Rooms and What They Symbolize

Room	Symbols Related to this Room's Function
Kitchen	Fresh foods, people preparing meals with gusto
Dining	People connecting over a shared meal
Bedroom	Relationships, personal or spiritual aspirations
Child's Room	Children's cherished dreams, heroes & heroines
Bathroom	Running water, purification, relaxation
Home Office	Career success and goals
Den	People conversing or studying
Music Room	Musicians playing, instrument images
Craft Room	Something made there, e.g. quilts or pottery
Workout Room	Fit, healthy, energetic people
Meditation Room	Altar, guru, saints, deities, inspiring scenes
Family Room	Family, ancestral memorabilia, celebrations

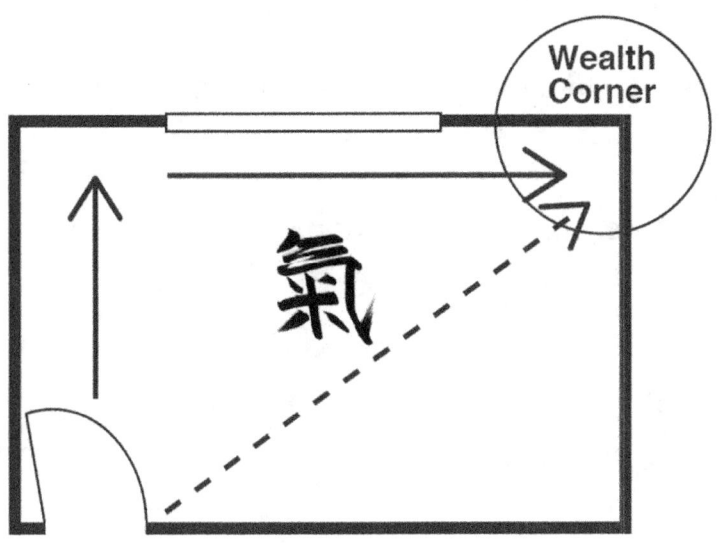

The Wealth Corner is a high focus area of a room at the farther diagonal corner. This illustration to the left is determined by the path and circulation of Qi (energy) in a room. Objects and images located in a wealth corner collect energy to manifest whatever the wealth corner objects symbolize.

What Are They Looking at Really?

A realty ad might read: "180-degree view, must see!" If accurate, all it means is that one side of a room has mostly windows. Everything out one side of the room is considered a view, somehow valuable just because you can look at it. We all know that everything you can see is not attractive, so when it comes to buildings why ignore that piece of visual wisdom? This is not so much a call to truth in realty advertising as it is a merchandising (and feng shui) pointer. The question is: of the viewable view, which part is essential? Why you want to know that is so you can show that with clarity to prospective buyers. The essential view is a potent selling point.

There are several ways to train yourself to see the essential view. If you have photographed a lot, you will have learned how to frame people, flowers, mountainsides, and buildings after tiring of taking photos that didn't do the subject justice. Framing is a discipline of getting rid of the extraneous. It's like pruning limbs in bonsai, or cutting flowers for ikebana.

Here is the procedure to see the essential view: Look out the window and identify the truly ugly. Mask the ugly out of the viewing field immediately by pulling shades, closing blinds, repositioning furniture or moving plants around. Look again. What is the most interesting or beautiful thing you can see? It may be a mountain, a blooming azalea or a snow laden bough of a juniper. Next, look at nearby objects and compare them to the most interesting object you saw. Do they enhance, detract or do nothing for the outward view? If they detract, hide that part of the view the same way you masked the downright ugly objects you initially fixed. What is left is the essential view, or near enough to it for the American housing market.

When you stage a house, just before the public is due for the open house showing, search out the essential view in each room. Position the curtains, blinds or shades in each room to highlight the essential view possible on that day, at that time, from that window or that vantage. If you find nothing beautiful outside, then trim the window blinds or pull the drapes so you highlight the inside of the room. It may be that all you want is light from the sky and not the view of the neighbor's weathered garage and compost heap. The essential view may be inside because of a marvelous red granite fireplace or masterful bird's-eye maple cabinets. If the outside view detracts from the inside view, close it off. In revealing the essential view, practice makes perfect and properties shown in their best light do sell.

CHAPTER 9

When Buildings Don't Sell

In a sellers' market, you don't have to do much to move a property. In a buyers' market, or with a disadvantaged building in any market, you have to do more work. Here we will consider what to do with difficult properties. In previous chapters, we presented a lot of good feng shui, common sense, relationship and business advice, all nicely integrated and ready to use. With hard to sell properties, you have to follow all the steps we've previously discussed before applying some of the more specific fixes set out here. Otherwise, you may have a common problem you just haven't attended to yet. So, as a quick recap, and for those who have jumped to this topic first out of economic desperation, here's a précis of the synopsis of the summary of 5,000 years of feng shui wisdom.

There are relationship, market, timing, and building problems. There are ghost and sci-fi type problems too, but we won't discuss them here because you encounter them much more rarely in experience. To solve them you can engage a psychic, physicist or priest. To solve the more common problems, you can use this outline to review where you are in the process:

1. Do your seller or buyer clients trust you? Do you trust them? Solution: Work on creating a relationship, a team spirit and trust as discussed in Chapter 2.

2. Does the building fit in with the established neighborhood pattern? Is it typical, different or very, very different? Solution: Make the façade at least look like it fits in the neighborhood but in a little bit better shape than its immediate neighbors.

3. Are the sellers more attached to the odor of their past or looking to let in the fresh air of change? Solution: Meet with the clients outside their home, and become a counselor, coaching them about how to activate the positive prospects of change in their lives.

4. Are the sellers directed by life goals or just moving from situation to situation as the winds of change blow? Solution: Get the clients to state their life goals, then focus them on skillfully using the change of residence or office as a direct step in activating those important goals.

5. For inhabited properties, what is the history of the place including how it was passed on to other residents by lease or deed of ownership? Solution: Re-use the pattern of sale transaction that has worked best in the past for this place as discussed in Chapter 4.

6. Are your clients ready to move on with their lives? Have you or your clients removed the subtle and not so subtle barriers to action? Solution: Use the common, but effective rituals discussed in Chapter 5 to accelerate the sale.

7. Is the decision-making process clear? Are the ultimate decision makers aware of the issues with the market and the property? Solution: Use meeting management skills, including feng shui

seating and location to lead the process to a productive conclusion as discussed in Chapter 6.

8. Are you or your clients at the wrong place at the wrong time? Are there no good reasons why things are bungling badly? Solution: Check out the astronomical and astrological conditions discussed in Chapter 7 to make sure you are propelled by and not fighting the flow of time.

9. Is it clear how to get in the building? Does the building warmly beckon or does it shun visitors? Solution: Use the principles in Chapter 8 to make the entrance active and attractive.

10. Do visitors not go into certain rooms that you want to showcase? Solution: Use the staging technique of creating a string of pearls on a cord of awareness as discussed in Chapter 8.

11. Have you or your clients arranged the wealth corners in the house to reflect their goals that changing places will help? Solution: Consult Chapter 8 for determining where wealth corners are and what sort of items to remove from them and to place in them.

If you have managed the above situations as well as you can, then it's time to see if any of the specific problems outlined below are holding you back. Keep in mind that whatever changes you make to the property, they need to be proportional, aesthetic, and in the same or compatible materials already used in the building or landscape. The best change is the one that no neighbor can remember when it was done because it looks like it always was that way.

T-squares: Some houses or business properties are located so that a street is aimed at them. At the last moment, the road veers right or left, but the accumulated energy continues straight ahead to disrupt things. This is the case in many cul-de-sacs in which one property is at the end. To protect the people living there, place a solid fence, or a large boulder to absorb the energy. As an alternative, a large fountain (about the width of half the attacking road and at least the height of a person) will continuously divert negative energy yet still allow direct sight of the building. Planting a warding-off tree or bush is a very short-term strategy, because the channeled energy that disrupts domestic life will also injure plants so that they will either grow sparsely, or die. The shorter the distance from the street to the building, the more solid the protection needs to be, whether fence or boulders.

Corner houses: Usually homes are protected by neighboring houses. At the end of a block, however, corner houses can suffer problems because they lack guardians. In crime statistics, they are robbed more frequently than other houses. Corner houses therefore need protection using natural and symbolic guardians. Where zoning allows, corner houses should have fences around the entire perimeter of their back and side yards. There should be a combination of rocks, bushes, trees and fences in the front yard to establish a clearly defined and protected border. Cacti, roses and other thorny type trees and shrubs are great as one row of defense. Symbolic guardians are statues placed near the gates or front door, such as a pair of *fu* dogs (dragon dogs) lions, warriors, warrior angels, gargoyles, fierce animals or other symbolic security guards. Paint the eyes of the symbolic guardians red and they will function ever better in warding off harm.

Bars: Some houses, for real or imagined reasons have had their doors and windows barred for security. Verify that there is still a need for the bars because neighborhoods change. If there isn't, remove bars as they also ward off potential buyers, to say nothing of the casual visitor. If bars are required because of a high-risk crime area, then ensure that the entire perimeter is protected consistently. Paint over the black bars so they look more like a decorative feature rather than the sign of a prison or risky place. Match the house trim colors, but choose a color that de-emphasizes the bars such as the color of the patina of copper, a sort of blue green. The decoration will invoke feelings of copper which induces a more expansive sense than the contractive feeling brought on by black iron bars.

Naked Backyards: When backyards are completely open, they provide no protection. They also allow life energy to run through rather than accumulate to nourish the property. Naked backyards are usually found in housing developments where by force of CC&R bad feng shui is shared by all. They are also present when there are interesting or spectacular views from the backyard. Most of the backyard needs to be enclosed by stone, wood, or living shrub fences. If there is a view, consult Chapter 8 about finding the essential view. Then fence in that which is not essential, leaving a better framing of the view out back.

Backed by Water: Having water in the form of a stream, river, pond, lake or ocean behind one's property is a special case of naked backyards. It is usually a negative feature that drains financial, relationship and health energy from the occupants. If the history of the house, past or present residents, shows little sign of this, it means there are other feng shui factors present which mitigate this effect. If the back yard has flooded, then change is required more urgently. This type of backyard needs to be enclosed. In fact, nesting gardens within gardens provide greater protection from loss of health, wealth and family from water at the rear. The larger the body of water, the more the feeling of enclosure needs to be in order to offset the draining effects. Backyard pools are not a problem unless they are negative edge pools in which it appears that the water is draining away to the rear horizon. Installing an aerating fountain in the pool will improve this situation.

House Numbers: Sometimes bad feng shui can be improved by changing the house number. As a number sequence, you want an overall rising arrangement, such as 26578 or 137. Eights are considered good because they hold a high yet maintainable state, whereas nines, though a high number, presage a great change before moving up to the next level. Fours, because they sound like the word for death in Chinese and Japanese, have come to be considered negative in Asia. In the older layer of Chinese cosmology, fours were associated with wealth. Mostly, even or yin numbers suggest stability and calm, whereas primarily odd or yang numbers suggest activity, effort and change. Finally, the sequence of numbers shows the cycle activity.

For instance, 625 means there are three phases in the cycle of this property. There is a six-year period followed by a two-year period followed by a five-year period. (The numbers can also refer to months.) If an owner is selling the 625 property in the sixth, eighth, or thirteenth year, there is a natural change due. If the sale is taking place in the second year, this indicates the sale will be out of phase and harder, but not impossible to accomplish.

Bad Neighbors: The fastest way to neutralize negativity coming from next door or from across the street neighbors is to face a mirror out toward the offensive party's property. The mirror only needs to be the size of a hand, but not more than 12 square inches. If the neighbor is extremely negative, in addition to the mirror, put statutes of protective guardians at a few key places along the common border. These guardians are warriors, gargoyles, fierce animals, saints, or high-energy rocks. The guardian chosen should be specific to transforming the particular kind of negativity the neighbor emits. A hateful neighbor, for instance, should be confronted by the loving, compassionate presence of Guan Yin Bodhisattva or Our Lady of Guadalupe. Use symbolic guardians that are meaningful to you from your own religious or philosophical background.

Wind: Some houses are sited at habitually windy places. Too much wind usually disrupts the lives and activities of its occupants. To ameliorate this condition, place wind chimes near the corners of the house that are more exposed to the wind. You have to experiment a bit to find the right place and pitch of sound the chimes or a single wind-bell will make. If the chimes are hung in the hardest wind, their sound may drive both neighbors and occupants to distraction, which is not the intent. Rather, the intent is to disperse negativity in soothing sound. If a lightweight metal chime is used, it will jingle in any breeze. If a heavy chime is used, only strong winds will move it enough to create sound. To create the right balance requires some trial and error experimentation.

Churches, Cemeteries, and Spooky Places: If a property faces a church, cemetery or other spooky place, it requires protection. Spooky places (SP) include: prisons, orphanages, nursing homes, hospitals, same day surgery centers, funeral homes, battlefields, zoos, dams, casinos, haunted houses, civic buildings, bridges, theatres, sports arenas, museums, regional malls, schools, liquor stores, amusement parks, manufacturing plants, electric generation plants, sewage treatment facilities, airports, military bases, guns and weapons stores and ranges, TV, radio or cell phone transmission towers, courthouses, and brothels. A spooky place is either a very large building or area that dwarfs surrounding buildings and residents in scale, or is a place in which very unusual and intense emotions or energies are unleashed by many people.

The hardest SP configuration is when the doorway of a house exactly opposes the doorway of the church, cemetery or other SP. To fix it, the property's door needs protection by interposing a fence or dense foliage and a new entry or gateway area needs to be created that is offset from the church door. Additionally, the walkway leading from the street to the property should make at least one turn along the way even if the SP's and house's doors are not precisely opposite one another. Being neighbors to an SP means creating layers of protection for the property yet still making the property entry clearly visible and inviting.

Disruptive EMFs: Buildings under electric lines, especially high-tension main lines, emit electromagnetic fields (EMF) that injure the health resiliency of humans, animals and many plants. Inside the house, computers, TV's and a host of electric and electronic devices also emit EMFs. You can buy a meter to measure the strength of the VLF (Very Low Frequency) and ELF (Extremely Low Frequency) fields. The EMFs are measured in units of milligauss, named after Carl Friedrich Gauss who researched this phenomenon. You need some scientific measure of this part of the electromagnetic spectrum in order to know if your interventions are in fact decreasing harmful EMF fields present on the property or not. There are also cell phone apps that measure EMFs.

Currently there are no safety EMF dosage standards accepted in the United States, although the World Health Organization and other countries do have standards. It's a bit like the link between smoking and cancer thirty years ago. Many people including smokers, lawyers, doctors, and tobacco executives could see the negative health impacts of smoking, but there was no definitive legal proof that was not challenged by a host of industry initiated lawsuits. The same situation applies to EMF's today. Sweden did the first national public policy study followed by an immediate abatement program to protect its people. You need to do your own research on EMF's and come to your own conclusion about how you may need to protect your health.

Cancers and a wide range of health problems are caused by various strength EMF radiations which seem to interfere with and suppress healthy immune system responses. With your nose against a TV set or your electric box, the EMF reading might be 100 or more milligauss (mg). Six to nine feet away from a source might drop the effect to 3 milligauss or less. There are unofficial studies that show that EMF fields of less than 3 milligauss are non-disruptive. Others, including our own experience, indicate that a safe field is 1 milligauss or less. These measures especially apply to places where a person would stand, sit, or recline for longer periods of time. So, if you can demonstrate to interested buyers that the EMF measures are low, even if all sorts of electric wires run into or closely parallel to the building, there is really no problem that honest salesmanship cannot counter.

When EMF measures exceed safe levels, it's time for action. You can experiment by grounding specific walls with totally non-conductive metals and materials. You can experiment with various products to protect a person or a building. You can create electronic nets that protect a home from harmful, outside electric fields. Because each place is unique, if you don't have EMF abatement expertise, you'll need to consult a specialist. An ordinary electrician will prove unsatisfactory as will a troubleshooter from the electric utility company. Each specialist, however, may be able to shed some light on the problem, and suggest a few possible solutions. In the most extreme case, where high-tension electric cables run close to the building in question, a piecemeal solution won't reverse the problem. To find a capable specialist, you may have to consult with an electrical engineering firm that specializes in creating zero charge environments as in the computer electronics market.

Dead Flora: When looking at landscaping, note where dead plants, trees, and shrubs dwell. Although it's important to remove the dead branches and plants with alacrity, first make certain you know what caused their demise. What you are looking to determine is whether a bush has died because of an injury, lack of watering or other easily remedied condition that can be avoided with the next replanting. Or, have you discovered an underlying earth condition that has caused the plant's demise, and most likely will do the same to the next replanting at that spot. Additionally, dead plants mean that there is some dysfunction in the area of life or work where the dead plant is near. Furthermore, the larger the dead or dying plant, the greater is the trouble it indicates. So, if a dead, fifty-foot scotch pine is right outside a master bedroom (whether you can see it through a window in that room or not), a couple's relationship is near the dead zone too. If the pine died because of neglect, there is hope for starting over. If, however, there is an underlying soil or earth problem, a fundamental life change is the only act that can recreate a healthy relationship.

Leaks: Where there are leaks, there is monetary drain. The more persistent and large the amount of water, oil or other fluid leaked, the greater is the indication of the drain on the household or business budget. Leaks secondarily can mean leaks of trust, health vitality, or focus. Whether the kitchen, bathroom, septic, pool, or irrigation system leaks it shows the likely origin of the loss, whether internal or external. A seller might be apt to avoid repairing leaks until a purchase offer is accepted and the property is in escrow. That is a poor feng shui strategy as it implies that at transaction's end less money will end up in the hands of the seller than should have. Fix leaks quickly and completely.

Fountains: Where there is little interest in a property or the purchase offers tendered are intolerably low, installing a flowing fountain in the front yard changes situations for the better. The fountain, when in flow needs to be proportionally sized, at least seven-eighths the height of the main entry door. If the entry is distant from the street, then a fountain with a louder, splashing sound will draw visitors with opportunities closer. The sound of any front yard fountain should be audible, but not overpowering when heard from the street. Flowing water purifies places and people so it becomes easier to let go of negative situations and move on freely. Flowing water attracts opportunities for wealth and prosperity. Flowing water also nourishes and heals the life force.

Dead or Red: Another tactic to attract interest in a seemingly dead property is to show the front entry area in glowing red. Paint the door or jamb red. Paint the trim red. Surround the entry in bougainvillea, roses, geraniums, or other red flowers. Red banners, kites, or wreaths adorning the doorway also draw attention to the places they grace. Red is important on earth because it is the color of the common blood of the human race. It is the color of transforming ideas and intents into action in the world. How much red is needed depends on how dark or hidden the entry is. In an easy to see entrance, just a sliver of red is enough to attract attention. In a darkly shaded, or strangely angled entrance, a wall of red may not be enough. Remember that the hue of red on the paint chip will not be the color seen from afar. For a dark area, choose a brighter red to compensate so the door is visible from the street.

Mirrored Foyers: There is a protective and a repulsive use of mirrors in the foyer. Placing a mirror directly opposite the front door as you enter is a repelling use. Mirrors bounce light and energy about as well as open vistas into eerie dream worlds. As a visitor moves toward the mirror, her own image will bounce back to repel her backwards. It creates a barrier to connection which is a poor result that counters your marketing effort to reach out to entice prospective buyers. The protective use of a foyer mirror uses the same bounce-back energy. A mirror placed on either the left or right wall relative to the entry is in a place of protection. This mirror placement creates a sort of barrier field to ward off negative incursions into the building. Mirrors placed and angled above the height of humans in order to reflect light and create an open feeling into the room is a neutral mirror use.

Fixing Faulty Foyers: This leads us to a consideration of foyers and the inside of entries. Since it is the first impression of inside, the entry needs to strike a delicate balance between two functions: pausing and inviting. If the foyer is too dark, restrictive, or heavy, then it will repulse people. If there is no transition between outside and inside, then anyone entering disrupts the household momentarily. So, the foyer must be able to hold visitors pleasantly and adjust them to the new environment. If it's full of more light or is more decorous than the rest of the house, visitors will be loath to enter the rest of the way. Square or rectangular foyer rugs signal pauses. Walls or screens placed to restrict the view on entry to the next room or two protects the household from outside intrusion. Placing some artwork in the foyer that sets the theme of the house helps establish adjustment and connection to the inside world. Finally, placing interesting artwork or furniture ensembles on the path to the next room will lead visitors where you want them to go next.

In, Then Shot Out Like an Arrow: A special case of bad entry occurs when a wall of large windows with sliding glass doors stands opposite the entry. This arrangement accelerates visitors out. If the backyard has no walls, the visitor ejection effect will be perfect and devastating. To check this, inquire into the current occupants' history, specifically if they have experienced a relative shortfall of money, lack of health, or lack of time spent enjoying their home. The pattern of their history shows where and how serious the situation of loss is. To fix the situation interpose a wall, tapestry or screen that blocks most of the view to the backyard until the visitor walks around the barrier. Also, keep curtains or blinds closed so that the view outside is decreased. At night, unless the back yard is well lit, completely close the window coverings to conserve household energy. If the backyard has no fence or a low fence, and the house is languishing on the market, then the seller needs to install at least a six-foot-high fence across the rear border of the property. A hedge fence that will grow to six feet or more in three years will not contribute to selling the house in the next three months.

Voodoo Art: Some people collect what is called primitive art. Often these are masks or ritual objects used by tribal shaman to attain some purpose, good or bad. These objets d'art have been invested with power and retain a portion of that power even outside the ritual or tribal context from which they emerged. In selling a house, the extra energies introduced by these shamanistic items just confuse the situation. If a ritual item has been designed specifically for a person or a house for protection, happiness or prosperity, then continue to display that piece as the home is being shown to prospective buyers. Remove all the other pieces from display, and preferably, store them off property.

Altars: Some people have created altars in their homes. Although as a realty agent, you might think this limits the market unduly by putting off prospective buyers, especially those who don't share the same philosophic or religious beliefs as the occupants. This is most often prudent advice. On the other hand, because the occupants have prayed, meditated, contemplated in a room where their altar is, they have gradually come to create and maintain an energy field. That field, if strong enough, may permeate the entire building or property. As a point of discussion, let us say that the intent of their religious practice is to generate and spread loving kindness and wisdom. As a feng shui marketing qualification, the party who succeeds in buying the property next will resonate positively to the energy field of wisdom and loving kindness. The next buyers may not express these aspirations the same way as the current owners, but nonetheless will respond positively to that energy and want to continue it in their own way. Recognize that the altar has become a vital center in this home, so instead of complete removal, you may ask the owners to screen it off when showing the house.

Fu translates as prosperity, good fortune, or luck. The character actually is a deeper expression. On the left side appears a character that shows spirit or alternately angels, guides or divine providence. The right side is composed of one, a mouth and a field. So, the pictorial meaning shows providence providing the bounty of an entire field of harvest for one person.

CHAPTER 10

Becoming More Feng Shui REALty Aware

What we have shared up to this point can be taken in several ways. The foregoing chapters are replete with methods to make the sale move more swiftly and harmoniously. We hope by applying feng shui insights in your real estate career you will indeed actualize greater prosperity and satisfaction for yourself and your loved ones. What we hope we have communicated are contours to the realty universe that you might not notice apart from a feng shui vantage. There are also lines of effective action that naturally flow from the feng shui view. Seeing and working with feng shui, coupled with what you already know as a real estate agent, geometrically increases the ways that you can skillfully and satisfactorily conclude any realty transaction.

One measure of success that real estate brokers track and that your business plan seeks to maximize is your own gross sales volume expressed in income. For your clients, the change of personal residence or business address has qualitative outcomes as well. For a family, success is measured by changes in health, happiness, learning, career, community, friendships, marriage, child rearing, sports, art, creativity and spiritual well-being including monetary wealth. Being a realty agent with a feng shui focus means attending to all these measures of your clients' success. It also means recognizing that you are contributing to the quality of your clients' entire lives not merely facilitating a deal to acquire one component of their estate.

Levels of Feng Shui: A popular view of feng shui is as a piecemeal set of tools to be tried when other initiatives and tactics fail. Popularly, hanging the odd crystal, doubling apparent room volume with mirrors or placing a red flower "just so" miss the potential feng shui has to integrate life as you move toward your goals with greater precision and alacrity. Although feng shui can operate with some success when employed with a patchwork mindset, you need to transcend this level of thinking. Using feng shui as a perspective with logic, method and application will take you to the next level of understanding. Treat it like a branch of science or mathematics complete with puzzles, experiments, tests, solutions and inventions. Then, compare your observations carefully to discover what is true about place (所).

The Chinese word "*xin*" ("*shin*" in Japanese) means a person's heart and mind together. There are three changes of your heart/mind that are usually necessary to move from patchwork feng shui to perspective feng shui. The first is simply that you have tried feng shui in the laboratory of your own home and office and found it to have helped you move forward in your life. At the start, you need someone knowledgeable to advise you of what to do. After that, as you learn more, you make feng shui experiments of your own. The second mind change is that you play with feng shui consistently. You look at the state of people's homes and offices and compare it to the condition of their current life experiences. You watch as others make feng shui changes and note the personal changes that happen after that. In this it pays to be more scientific matching causes with effects. The third heart/mind change is a watershed event that happens after you've critically watched feng shui for some time.

Some afternoon as you tilt back in your chair sipping a cup of Ethiopian coffee, taking a break from the reading PDF files on your desktop monitor, you put your mind in neutral for just a moment of peace. Unbidden, the overall pattern hits you: the configuration of people's homes and offices really does correlate with how they act. And strangely, almost fantastically, you know that when you or they change something inside, a response change really happens in life experience outside. It's really true! There is an intricate ballet of inside change invoking and leading to outside change. Once this realization is firm in your awareness, you will never view the workings of the world the same again. Although you may not have resolved all the questions you have about specific points of feng shui, or found your experiments to be 100% accurate, what you know is that the perspective is valid. You also know that you cannot ignore something this important.

There are some people who from their earliest intuitions have known that the energies of time and place change and effect people's lives. What makes this knowledge a lonesome science is that the majority of people don't see this cause/effect correlation at work behind the scenes of their lives shaping and altering their thoughts, emotions and actions. Once you really behold it, you realize how obvious it is. Once feng shui moves from the background as a quaint topic for social occasions to an obvious worldview, you have moved to the second level and understand feng shui as a perspective.

The next realization that dawns along the way in working with feng shui is that you as a realty agent, interior designer, architect, contractor, furnishings salesman or landscaper have a hand in bringing people closer to disappointment or more toward their hearts' delights. This is not to say a person isn't primarily responsible for his or her own decisions and life path. What it does mean is that there is no impersonal random order at work in the great cosmos, nor at work in any individual life within the cosmos. It means that lives move together forward or backward. This view of the intricate, interrelated web of life brings everyone to the same impasse. One solution is not to explore this view any longer by denying that the welfare of one person intimately effects the welfare of us all. The other solution leads to compassionate action towards every being with feelings, including the earth herself.

How you choose to meet the web of life leaves you to operate at the second level of feng shui or elevate to the third level of caring feng shui. It is higher not because it will increase profitability, but because in order to practice it you have to move beyond yourself. In so doing your intent is to help the entire web of living beings, not just yourself. To commit to help all beings on the same web is to work on a grander order of the cosmos. That is why this next level is a higher feng shui. When the same wind blows, it touches everyone. When the clouds come, the same water rains on everyone.

Practical Beginnings: If you've read this and other books on feng shui you've already taken the first step. You now know a number of ways to diagnose common problems and several specific remedies for them. As you progress in your own investigation you will want to learn more to broaden your store of knowledge. An incredible advantage that a seasoned real estate agent or anyone else in the building industry has is a large personal database of property specific experiences. If you want to learn feng shui rapidly, review the various realty transactions that you have made. Next, recall the features of the houses or other properties that you've worked with. Note a few details of feng shui that stand out at each place. Next, and this may require follow-up, check with each family or firm and simply chat about what has happened to them since they moved in. What are the major setbacks, accomplishments and prospects now? Finally, correlate the feng shui details with the events and changes that have happened to test the feng shui view.

Your own personal experiential evidence is the most convincing of any proof or disproof that you can encounter. In order to learn this way though, you need to be thorough. Make a feng shui journal for yourself in which you can record your findings. Just take notes that make sense to you. You may want to start with the most recent cases and work backwards through time. As you record cases, you'll want to correlate the following information:

Case History Review Journal

1. Clients' names & brief personal history

2. History of the house they were about to move to, if any

3. Description of building noting unusual features

4. Description of furniture arrangement and artworks

5. Your feng shui evaluation of the place

6. History of the family since they moved in (see Chapter 3)

7. What remodeling if any has been done since the move in

8. How did the events match or fall short of your feng shui expectations

9. What was puzzling, extreme or unexpected

Take various photos to put with your journal. It will save jotting a lot of notes. Besides, when you review your notes, you will undoubtedly spot photo details you didn't notice before. If you already keep such a journal of your work for marketing purposes, then you'll have even less work as more rapidly you review and learn. Actually, by dealing in real estate every day, it should be simple to learn because you don't have to go out of your way at all. Clients, their personalities, their goals, their histories, potential properties, the selection and purchase process are all in the natural flow of the realty business. Marketing follow-up is also a natural part. Reviewing your past experiences so you see the feng shui side of the experiences makes the ideal next step for any professional who deals with people and buildings to learn feng shui.

Developing What You Know About Feng Shui: Once you've finished this review, even if you've only picked eight property client case histories to study (including your own), you will have a good foundation not because you have all the necessary feng shui knowledge but because you've gained insight. At the end of your review process you will see that you do need more information. Your results will point you in the directions in which you need to go to fill in the gaps in your data. To get a good overall introduction to feng shui and a life framework for learning and integrating feng shui, refer to the book: *Feng Shui: The Art and Harmony of Place*, by Johndennis Govert.

Over the past thirty years we've taught feng shui in living rooms, bookstores, libraries, museums, restaurants, community colleges, design conferences, body work schools, acupuncture colleges, churches and spiritual centers. Consequently, we've developed a sense of the breadth of information we can impart in about thirty hours of feng shui instruction. The purpose of this book is not to cover everything you'll ever want to know about feng shui, but to get you started now, and to point you in the right direction for lifelong learning.

Beyond Data: After seeing a lot of possible feng shui data you might one day learn, don't be daunted. There are compatible and parallel ways to develop because information is useless unless you can apply it. The average citizen has to be content learning and practicing feng shui upon unsuspecting neighbors, relatives and friends. They are restricted in encountering practical outlets for their feng shui experimentation. Realty agents are not. You have many more opportunities to learn by practice to see what works, what doesn't, and what's confusing. That leaves only three other avenues to develop.

Harmony: The first is a sense of aesthetics. Some people already have the feeling for how to achieve proportion, beauty, and harmony. Some do not. Whatever innate aesthetics talent you already have, you can always develop it further. One of the lessons of the development of Chinese feng shui in Japan is that all the feng shui principles had to be incorporated into the overall Japanese aesthetic of a room, garden or house. Right feng shui equates to natural patterns of beauty that we replicate in our dwellings. A good feng shui feature is one that fits seamlessly into the patterns and colors of an existing setting, yet creates or focuses positive energy. It's not really in the scope of this book to discuss ways to develop aesthetic sensibilities, but rather, to remind you that feng shui changes have to fit harmoniously into the whole if we plan to live with them and see them every day. We have discovered that people who have highly developed aesthetic senses, often, but not always, create positive feng shui arrangements.

Intuition: The next faculty to develop that helps not only in feng shui but in every area of life is intuition. To some, intuition means ESP or psychic talent. That is indeed part of it. Remember that psychic or ESP talent is part of the nature of all human perception.

It's there sleeping, and it can be awakened. Another part of intuition, we can develop from experience. An example from sports is a basketball player on a fast break can sense another player from behind without seeing him. The first player also knows where the second player is, how fast he's moving and what's his intention. So, in various areas of our lives, we develop so much experience that we are able to fill in the gaps accurately. That too is trained intuition. Intuition can be developed through the meditative and performing arts. The easiest way to open our intuitive channels is to engage in any act of creativity. A creative mindset leads to intuitive perception and action. The more usual it is for any of us to dwell in a creative perspective, the more usual it is that we will use our intuitions well to integrate our experiences and aspirations connected to an understanding of place (所).

Xin is character for mind and heart as one. It is drawn with four brush strokes perhaps one for each chamber of the physical heart.

Heart: If we develop the intent to benefit someone through feng shui, whatever changes we might suggest will create some positive outcome for that person. This applies to any of our endeavors in life. The more considerate we are of the welfare of others, who seek the same happiness that we ourselves seek, the more we will be able to benefit them directly or indirectly. Developing a loving heart is usually the province of religion and philosophy. Its chief hallmark is the ability to tend to the interests of others even when those interests occasionally run contrary to our own short-term interests. The sincerer our concern for others, the greater is our ability to benefit them. In feng shui terms it may be only to connect them with someone who can solve the unusual specifics of the problem that brings you or your client suffering. Developing a loving and caring heart leads to the highest level of practice of the science and art of feng shui or realty.

We so often hear of people searching for or constructing not so much their dream offices, but their dream homes. When questioned about how satisfied home owners are with what they have found, remodeled or constructed, often we find great disappointment. The dream somehow became confused along the way. Each of us has dreams for our lives and objectives for our living spaces. The feng shui process is to transform your home into a wish fulfilling gem. That means as you make changes to improve your living environment, you should also, and more importantly, move with greater ease toward accomplishing your life goals. When home owners meet great resistance in their lives and experience unusual blocks to achieving their goals and their happiness, something is very amiss with their home. It doesn't matter whether little or great thought or effort went into acquiring a home that doesn't deliver on life aspirations. Becoming more skillful as a feng shui realty agent is about helping clients discover and use their homes as wish fulfilling gems to bring greater fulfillment into every corner of their lives.

APPENDIX 1

Solar and Lunar Eclipses 2015 to 2025

Luminary	Type	Date	Degree & Sign
Solar	Central Total	Mar 20 2015	29° Pisces 27'
Lunar	Total	Apr 04 2015	14° Libra 24'
Solar	Partial	Sep 12 2015	20° Virgo 10'
Lunar	Total	Sep 27 2015	04° Aries 40'
Solar	Central Total	Mar 08 2016	18° Pisces 55'
Lunar	Penumbral	Mar 23 2016	03° Libra 17'
Lunar	Almost	Aug 18 2016	25° Aquarius 51'
Solar	Central Annular	Sep 01 2016	09° Virgo 01'
Lunar	Penumbral	Sep 16 2016	24° Pisces 19'
Lunar	Penumbral	Feb 10 2017	22° Leo 28'
Solar	Central Annular	Feb 26 2017	08° Pisces 12'
Lunar	Penumbral	Aug 07 2017	15° Aquarius 25'
Solar	Central Total	Aug 21 2017	28° Leo 52'
Lunar	Total	Jan 31 2018	11° Leo 37'
Solar	Partial	Feb 15 2018	27° Aquarius 07'
Solar	Partial	Jul 12 2018	20° Cancer 41'
Lunar	Total	Jul 27 2018	04° Aquarius 44'
Solar	Partial	Aug 11 2018	18° Leo 41'
Solar	Partial	Jan 05 2019	15° Capricorn 25'
Lunar	Total	Jan 20 2019	00° Leo 51'
Solar	Central Total	Jul 02 2019	10° Cancer 37'

Luminary	Type	Date	Degree & Sign
Lunar	Partial	Jul 16 2019	24° Capricorn 04'
Solar	Central Annular	Dec 25 2019	04° Capricorn 06'
Lunar	Penumbral	Jan 10 2020	20° Cancer 00'
Solar	Central Annular	Jun 20 2020	00° Cancer 21'
Lunar	Penumbral	Jun 05 2020	15° Sagittarius 34'
Lunar	Penumbral	Jul 04 2020	13° Capricorn 37'
Lunar	Penumbral	Nov 30 2020	08° Gemini 38'
Solar	Central Total	Dec 14 2020	23° Sagittarius 08'
Lunar	Total	May 26 2021	05° Sagittarius 25'
Solar	Central Annular	Jun 10 2021	19° Gemini 47'
Lunar	Partial	Nov 19 2021	27° Taurus 14'
Solar	Central Total	Dec 04 2021	12° Sagittarius 22'
Solar	Partial	Apr 30 2022	10° Taurus 28'
Lunar	Total	May 15 2022	25° Scorpio 17'
Solar	Partial	Oct 25 2022	02° Scorpio 00'
Lunar	Total	Nov 08 2022	16° Taurus 00'
Solar	Central Annular Total	Apr 19 2023	29° Aries 50'
Lunar	Penumbral	May 05 2023	14° Scorpio 58'
Solar	Central Annular	Oct 14 2023	21° Libra 07'
Lunar	Partial	Oct 28 2023	05° Taurus 09'
Lunar	Penumbral	Mar 25 2024	05° Libra 07'
Solar	Central Total	Apr 08 2024	19° Aries 24'
Lunar	Partial	Sep 17 2024	25° Pisces 40'
Solar	Central Annular	Oct 02 2024	10° Libra 03'
Lunar	Total	Mar 13 2025	23° Virgo 56'
Solar	Partial	Mar 29 2025	09° Aries 00'
Lunar	Total	Sep 07 2025	15° Pisces 22'
Solar	Partial	Sep 21 2025	29° Virgo 05'

Solar eclipse types are central total, central annular and partial listed from most impact on behavior to lesser. In a central total solar eclipse the moon completely covers and darkens the entire solar disc creating a path of total shadow across an arc on earth. In a central annular eclipse, the moon is at its farthest distance from earth, and almost covers the sun. It leaves a ring of fire along the outer edge of the visible sun. In a partial solar eclipse seen from earth, some crescent of the sun shines visibly while the rest of the sun's disc is dark.

Lunar eclipse types are total, penumbral and partial, also listed from most impact on behavior to lesser impact. The darkest part of the earth's shadow on the moon is called the umbra. When the moon is totally within the umbra, then the moon is totally eclipsed. The earth can also cast a lighter shadow on the moon called the penumbra. The moon partly or completely appearing in this lighter shadow creates a penumbral eclipse. Finally, when a crescent shadow of the earth crosses the moon so that the moon shows a dark crescent and a lighter part together, this is an example of a partial lunar eclipse.

APPENDIX 2

Planetary Direction Changes 2015 to 2025

Planet	Motion*	2015 Date	Degree & Sign
Mercury	SR	Jan 21 2015	17° Aquarius 05'
Mercury	SD	Feb 11 2015	01° Aquarius 18'
Saturn	SR	Mar 14 2015	04° Sagittarius 55'
Jupiter	SD	Apr 08 2015	12° Leo 35'
Pluto	SR	Apr 16 2015	15° Capricorn 32'
Mercury	SR	May 18 2015	13° Gemini 08'
Mercury	SD	Jun 11 2015	04° Gemini 33'
Neptune	SR	Jun 12 2015	09° Pisces 49'
Venus	SR	Jul 25 2015	00° Virgo 46'
Uranus	SR	Jul 26 2015	20° Aries 30'
Saturn	SD	Aug 01 2015	28° Scorpio 16'
Venus	SD	Sep 06 2015	14° Leo 23'
Mercury	SR	Sep 17 2015	15° Libra 55'
Pluto	SD	Sep 24 2015	12° Capricorn 58'
Mercury	SD	Oct 09 2015	00° Libra 53'
Neptune	SD	Nov 18 2015	07° Pisces 01'
Uranus	SD	Dec 25 2015	16° Aries 33'

*SR indicates that a planet appears to become stationary in the sky and appears about to move backwards or in retrograde motion.

*SD indicates that a planet appears to become stationary just before appearing to move forwards or in direct motion.

Stationary is an equivalent term for standstill.

Planet	Motion*	2016 Date	Degree & Sign
Mercury	SRx	Jan 05 2016	01° Aquarius 02'
Jupiter	SRx	Jan 07 2016	23° Virgo 14'
Mercury	SD	Jan 25 2016	14° Capricorn 54'
Saturn	SRx	Mar 25 2016	16° Sagittarius 24'
Mars	SRx	Apr 17 2016	08° Sagittarius 54'
Pluto	SRx	Apr 18 2016	17° Capricorn 29'
Mercury	SRx	Apr 28 2016	23° Taurus 36'
Jupiter	SD	May 09 2016	23° Virgo 14'
Mercury	SD	May 22 2016	14° Taurus 20'
Neptune	SRx	Jun 13 2016	12° Pisces 02'
Mars	SD	Jun 29 2016	23° Scorpio 03'
Uranus	SRx	Jul 29 2016	24° Aries 30'
Saturn	SD	Aug 13 2016	09° Sagittarius 46'
Mercury	SRx	Aug 30 2016	29° Virgo 04'
Mercury	SD	Sep 21 2016	14° Virgo 49'
Pluto	SD	Sep 26 2016	14° Capricorn 55'
Neptune	SD	Nov 19 2016	09° Pisces 14'
Mercury	SRx	Dec 19 2016	15° Capricorn 07'
Uranus	SD	Dec 29 2016	20° Aries 33'

Planet	Motion*	2017 Date	Degree & Sign
Mercury	SD	Jan 08 2017	28° Sagittarius 50'
Jupiter	SRx	Feb 05 2017	23° Libra 08'
Venus	SRx	Mar 04 2017	13° Aries 08'
Saturn	SRx	Apr 05 2017	27° Sagittarius 47'
Mercury	SRx	Apr 09 2017	04° Taurus 50'
Venus	SD	Apr 15 2017	26° Pisces 54'
Pluto	SRx	Apr 20 2017	19° Capricorn 23'
Mercury	SD	May 03 2017	24° Aries 15'
Jupiter	SD	Jun 09 2017	13° Libra 12'

Planet	Motion*	2017 Date	Degree & Sign
Neptune	SRx	Jun 16 2017	14° Pisces 15'
Uranus	SRx	Aug 02 2017	28° Aries 31'
Mercury	SRx	Aug 12 2017	11° Virgo 38'
Saturn	SD	Aug 25 2017	21° Sagittarius 10'
Mercury	SD	Sep 05 2017	28° Leo 25'
Pluto	SD	Sep 28 2017	16° Capricorn 51'
Neptune	SD	Nov 22 2017	11° Pisces 27'
Mercury	SRx	Dec 03 2017	29° Sagittarius 18'
Mercury	SD	Dec 22 2017	13° Sagittarius 00'

Planet	Motion*	2018 Date	Degree & Sign
Uranus	SD	Jan 02 2018	24° Aries 34'
Jupiter	SRx	Mar 08 2018	23° Scorpio 13'
Mercury	SRx	Mar 22 2018	16° Aries 54'
Mercury	SD	Apr 15 2018	04° Aries 46'
Saturn	SRx	Apr 17 2018	09° Capricorn 08'
Pluto	SRx	Apr 22 2018	21° Capricorn 17'
Neptune	SRx	Jun 18 2018	16° Pisces 29'
Mars	SRx	Jun 26 2018	09° Aquarius 13'
Jupiter	SD	Jul 10 2018	13° Scorpio 20'
Mercury	SRx	Jul 25 2018	23° Leo 27'
Uranus	SRx	Aug 07 2018	02° Taurus 33'
Mercury	SD	Aug 18 2018	11° Leo 31'
Mars	SD	Aug 27 2018	28° Capricorn 36'
Saturn	SD	Sep 06 2018	02° Capricorn 32'
Pluto	SD	Sep 30 2018	18° Capricorn 45'
Venus	SRx	Oct 05 2018	10° Scorpio 50'
Venus	SD	Nov 16 2018	25° Libra 14'
Mercury	SRx	Nov 16 2018	13° Sagittarius 29'
Neptune	SD	Nov 24 2018	13° Pisces 41'
Mercury	SD	Dec 06 2018	27° Scorpio 16'

Planet	Motion*	2019 Date	Degree & Sign
Uranus	SD	Jan 06 2019	28° Aries 36'
Mercury	SRx	Mar 05 2019	29° Pisces 38'
Mercury	SD	Mar 28 2019	16° Pisces 05'
Jupiter	SRx	Apr 10 2019	24° Sagittarius 21'
Pluto	SRx	Apr 24 2019	23° Capricorn 09'
Saturn	SRx	Apr 29 2019	20° Capricorn 31'
Neptune	SRx	Jun 21 2019	18° Pisces 43'
Mercury	SRx	Jul 07 2019	04° Leo 27'
Mercury	SD	Jul 31 2019	23° Cancer 56'
Jupiter	SD	Aug 11 2019	14° Sagittarius 30'
Uranus	SRx	Aug 11 2019	06° Taurus 36'
Saturn	SD	Sep 18 2019	13° Capricorn 54'
Pluto	SD	Oct 02 2019	20° Capricorn 38'
Mercury	SRx	Oct 31 2019	27° Scorpio 38'
Mercury	SD	Nov 20 2019	11° Scorpio 35'
Neptune	SD	Nov 27 2019	15° Pisces 55'

Planet	Motion*	2020 Date	Degree & Sign
Uranus	SD	Jan 10 2020	02° Taurus 38'
Mercury	SRx	Feb 16 2020	12° Pisces 53'
Mercury	SD	Mar 09 2020	28° Aquarius 12'
Pluto	SRx	Apr 25 2020	24° Capricorn 59'
Saturn	SRx	May 10 2020	01° Aquarius 57'
Venus	SRx	May 12 2020	21° Gemini 50'
Jupiter	SRx	May 14 2020	27° Capricorn 14'
Mercury	SRx	Jun 17 2020	14° Cancer 45'
Neptune	SRx	Jun 22 2020	20° Pisces 57'
Venus	SD	Jun 24 2020	05° Gemini 20'
Mercury	SD	Jul 12 2020	05° Cancer 29'
Uranus	SRx	Aug 15 2020	10° Taurus 41'

Planet	Motion*	2020 Date	Degree & Sign
Mars	SRx	Sep 09 2020	28° Aries 08'
Jupiter	SD	Sep 12 2020	17° Capricorn 24'
Saturn	SD	Sep 28 2020	25° Capricorn 20'
Pluto	SD	Oct 04 2020	22° Capricorn 29'
Mercury	SRx	Oct 13 2020	11° Scorpio 40'
Mercury	SD	Nov 03 2020	25° Libra 53'
Mars	SD	Nov 13 2020	15° Aries 13'
Neptune	SD	Nov 28 2020	18° Pisces 09'

Planet	Motion*	2021 Date	Degree & Sign
Uranus	SD	Jan 14 2021	06° Taurus 43'
Mercury	SRx	Jan 30 2021	26° Aquarius 29'
Mercury	SD	Feb 20 2021	11° Aquarius 01'
Pluto	SRx	Apr 27 2021	26° Capricorn 48'
Saturn	SRx	May 23 2021	13° Aquarius 31'
Mercury	SRx	May 29 2021	24° Gemini 43'
Jupiter	SRx	Jun 20 2021	02° Pisces 11'
Mercury	SD	Jun 22 2021	16° Gemini 07'
Neptune	SRx	Jun 25 2021	23° Pisces 11'
Uranus	SRx	Aug 19 2021	14° Taurus 47'
Mercury	SRx	Sep 26 2021	25° Libra 28'
Pluto	SD	Oct 06 2021	24° Capricorn 18'
Saturn	SD	Oct 10 2021	06° Aquarius 52'
Jupiter	SD	Oct 17 2021	22° Aquarius 19'
Mercury	SD	Oct 18 2021	10° Libra 07'
Neptune	SD	Dec 01 2021	20° Pisces 24'
Venus	SRx	Dec 19 2021	26° Capricorn 29'

Planet	Motion*	2022 Date	Degree & Sign
Mercury	SRx	Jan 14 2022	10° Aquarius 20'
Uranus	SD	Jan 18 2022	10° Taurus 49'
Venus	SD	Jan 29 2022	11° Capricorn 04'
Mercury	SD	Feb 03 2022	24° Capricorn 22'
Pluto	SRx	Apr 29 2022	28° Capricorn 35'
Mercury	SRx	May 10 2022	04° Gemini 51'
Mercury	SD	Jun 03 2022	26° Taurus 05'
Saturn	SRx	Jun 04 2022	25° Aquarius 15'
Neptune	SRx	Jun 28 2022	25° Pisces 26'
Jupiter	SRx	Jul 28 2022	08° Aries 43'
Uranus	SRx	Aug 24 2022	18° Taurus 55'
Mercury	SRx	Sep 09 2022	08° Libra 55'
Mercury	SD	Oct 02 2022	24° Virgo 11'
Pluto	SD	Oct 08 2022	26° Capricorn 06'
Saturn	SD	Oct 22 2022	18° Aquarius 35'
Mars	SRx	Oct 30 2022	25° Gemini 36'
Jupiter	SD	Nov 23 2022	28° Pisces 47'
Neptune	SD	Dec 03 2022	22° Pisces 38'
Mercury	SRx	Dec 29 2022	24° Capricorn 21'

Planet	Motion*	2023 Date	Degree & Sign
Mars	SD	Jan 12 2023	08° Gemini 07'
Mercury	SD	Jan 18 2023	08° Capricorn 08'
Uranus	SD	Jan 22 2023	14° Taurus 56'
Mercury	SRx	Apr 21 2023	15° Taurus 37'
Pluto	SRx	May 01 2023	00° Aquarius 21'
Mercury	SD	May 14 2023	05° Taurus 50'
Saturn	SRx	Jun 17 2023	07° Pisces 12'
Neptune	SRx	Jun 30 2023	27° Pisces 41'
Venus	SRx	Jul 22 2023	28° Leo 36'

Planet	Motion*	2023 Date	Degree & Sign
Mercury	SRx	Aug 23 2023	21° Virgo 51'
Uranus	SRx	Aug 28 2023	23° Taurus 04'
Venus	SD	Sep 03 2023	12° Leo 12'
Jupiter	SRx	Sep 04 2023	15° Taurus 34'
Mercury	SD	Sep 15 2023	08° Virgo 00'
Pluto	SD	Oct 10 2023	27° Capricorn 53'
Saturn	SD	Nov 04 2023	00° Pisces 30'
Neptune	SD	Dec 06 2023	24° Pisces 53'
Mercury	SRx	Dec 13 2023	08° Capricorn 29'
Jupiter	SD	Dec 30 2023	05° Taurus 34'

Planet	Motion*	2024 Date	Degree & Sign
Mercury	SD	Jan 01 2024	22° Sagittarius 10'
Uranus	SD	Jan 27 2024	19° Taurus 05'
Mercury	SRx	Apr 01 2024	27° Aries 13'
Mercury	SD	Apr 25 2024	15° Aries 58'
Pluto	SRx	May 02 2024	02° Aquarius 06'
Saturn	SRx	Jun 29 2024	19° Pisces 25'
Neptune	SRx	Jul 02 2024	29° Pisces 55'
Mercury	SRx	Aug 04 2024	04° Virgo 06'
Mercury	SD	Aug 28 2024	21° Leo 24'
Uranus	SRx	Sep 01 2024	27° Taurus 15'
Jupiter	SRx	Oct 09 2024	21° Gemini 20'
Pluto	SD	Oct 11 2024	29° Capricorn 38'
Saturn	SD	Nov 15 2024	12° Pisces 41'
Mercury	SRx	Nov 25 2024	22° Sagittarius 40'
Mars	SRx	Dec 06 2024	06° Leo 10'
Neptune	SD	Dec 07 2024	27° Pisces 07'
Mercury	SD	Dec 15 2024	06° Sagittarius 23'

Planet	Motion*	2025 Date	Degree & Sign
Uranus	SD	Jan 30 2025	23° Taurus 15'
Jupiter	SD	Feb 04 2025	11° Gemini 16'
Mars	SD	Feb 23 2025	17° Cancer 00'
Venus	SR℞	Mar 01 2025	10° Aries 50'
Mercury	SR℞	Mar 14 2025	09° Aries 35'
Mercury	SD	Apr 07 2025	26° Pisces 49'
Venus	SD	Apr 12 2025	24° Pisces 37'
Pluto	SR℞	May 04 2025	03° Aquarius 49'
Neptune	SR℞	Jul 04 2025	02° Aries 10'
Saturn	SR℞	Jul 12 2025	01° Aries 56'
Mercury	SR℞	Jul 17 2025	15° Leo 34'
Mercury	SD	Aug 11 2025	04° Leo 14'
Uranus	SR℞	Sep 05 2025	01° Gemini 27'
Pluto	SD	Oct 13 2025	01° Aquarius 22'
Mercury	SR℞	Nov 09 2025	06° Sagittarius 51'
Jupiter	SR℞	Nov 11 2025	25° Cancer 09'
Saturn	SD	Nov 27 2025	25° Pisces 09'
Mercury	SD	Nov 29 2025	20° Scorpio 42'
Neptune	SD	Dec 10 2025	29° Pisces 22'

GLOSSARY

Terms defined in the glossary are for your convenience and come from various Asian languages. The language key is Chinese (CHN), Japanese (JPN), Sanskrit (SKT), and Tibetan (TBT). The abbreviations identify the language of origin.

***Aum Moni Pomo Long Hung*, or *Aum Mani Padme Hung*:** (CHN/SKT/TBT) "Hail to the Jewel in the Lotus!" This is a mantra invoking *Avalokiteshvara*, Bodhisattva of Compassion and one's own inner compassion. This is Master Quan's higher order version.

***Aum Oh May Doh Bu Sui*:** (SKT/CHN) This is the invocation to *Amitabha*, the Limitless Light Buddha. This is Master Quan's higher order version of **Aum Ami Dewa Hri.** (TBT)

***Ba gua*:** (CHN) The eight signs or trigrams of the I Ching representing eight natural and primal forces shaping the world.

Bodhisattva: (SKT) An enlightened being who remains in the cycle of human existence to help humans awake and evolve.

Buddhism: (SKT) A mystical practice concerned with cultivating Enlightenment. It began in India with the teachings of the historical Buddha, Gautama Siddhartha, and was transmitted throughout Asia. It is one of the three great philosophical schools of China.

Confucius, also ***Kung Fu Tzu*:** (CHN) Master Kung Fu, known by his Latinized title as Confucius, was founder of one of the three great philosophical schools of China.

Cosmological Feng Shui: This is a feng shui school that considers astrological conditions as well as cardinal directions and angles of structures and landscapes. This school uses the compass. See *Luo Pan*.

Dan Tian or Tanden: (CHN) (JPN) "Heavenly Field." Refers to psychic and energy centers of the body. The three main, *dan tian* energy centers are the navel, heart and area between the eyes.

Dao: (CHN) "The Way" is the mysterious and subtle origin of all reality and refers to paths of self-cultivation. It may also refer to an individual art of self-cultivation such as poetry, tea ceremony or, feng shui.

Dao De Jing: (CHN) *The Classic of the Way and Its Power*, a work attributed to Lao Tzu; the first written work in the Chinese Daoist school. **Do:** (JPN) is the Japanese pronunciation of *Dao*.

Daoism: (CHN) One of China's three great philosophical schools. Daoism has philosophical, mystical practice and religious sub-schools, and is based on Lao Tzu's teachings in the poems of the *Dao De Ching*.

Dharma: (SKT) "Universal law, duty, things." In both Vedic and Buddhist traditions, the teachings on the nature of universal law and the method of how to transform and transcend the small self.

Enso: (JPN) A circle drawn in calligraphy to represent the oneness of all life and to express intimate and immediate connection with the origin.

Feng Shui: (CHN) This means Wind Water and refers to the subtle to obvious spectrum of effects in every environment that influences the behavior of all those moving within a place (所).

Feng Shui Dao: (CHN) The Way of Wind and Water, is a feng shui school and method for self-cultivation that seeks to create advantage for all sides simultaneously.

Five Elements, also the **Wu Xing:** (CHN) This is also known as the five agents, and refers to the five basic processes at work in the world called wood, fire, earth, metal and water. The five Greek elements were called earth, water, fire, air and space.

Gua (sometimes *kua*): (CHN) Refers to one of eight trigrams or one of the sixty-four hexagrams found in the *I Ching*.

Huang Di: (CHN) The Yellow Emperor. The legendary first Emperor of China from the start of whose reign in 2698 BC, the Chinese years are counted. (Chinese year 4715 equals 2017 AD).

I Ching or **Yi Jing:** (CHN) *The Book of Change* is the oldest writing in China on philosophy, divination, culture and self-development.

Ikebana: (JPN) "The Way of Flower Arranging." Many styles and schools of this art flourish in Japan.

Kanji: (JPN) Chinese ideographic characters drawn with brush and ink.

Laoshi: (CHN) "Old Teacher," a title of respect. *Roshi* in Japanese.

Lao Tzu: (CHN) "Old Master." It refers to the author of the *Dao De Ching* and founder of Daoism, one of the three great philosophical schools of China.

Luo Pan: (CHN) A feng shui compass used by the cosmological school.

Mahayana: (SKT) "Great Vehicle." A branch of Buddhist practice that extols the attainment of enlightenment not only to relieve one's own suffering, but as a means to liberate and help others as well.

Mandala: (SKT) "Circle, orb." A symbolic seed representation in the center of a circular figure surrounded by concentric symbols showing how the universe is ordered. It is used in art or visualization meditation to enter into greater harmony or integration with the One.

Mantra: (SKT) Chanted or intoned sound vibrations to invoke positive and transforming thought forms to change internal and external conditions.

Master Quan Guan Liang: A Master of Tibetan Buddhism of the Nyingma school. He was the disciple of *Senton Dorje*, and the revered guru of the authors.

Ming Shu: (CHN) A system of Chinese astrology with applications used in the school of cosmological feng shui.

Pinyin: (CHN) A modem system for writing Chinese words in Roman letters developed in the PRC.

Power Feng Shui: This is a school of feng shui that uses all the characteristics of place to gain advantage for self and disadvantage for others. It is connected to the writings on the Art of War. See *Sun Tzu*.

Qi: (CHN) Sometimes written chi, this refers to basic life energy that flows through the body and the whole universe and mediates change between physical matter and emotional and mental realms. It is also referred to as ki in Korean and Japanese, *lung* in Tibetan and *prana* in Sanskrit.

Qi gong: (CHN) (Also *Ch'i Gung* or *Ch'i Kung*) Practice of internal exercises that promote accumulation and circulation of *qi* in the physical, astral and causal bodies. An indispensable practice in order to master any of the Arts or Ways.

Retrograde Planetary Motion: In astronomy and astrology, this refers to a period of time when a planet appears to move slowly backward in the sky before resuming its usual and direct motion forward.

River Lo Map: (CHN) Also known as the River Lo Writing, it is an ancient written text used in the yin-yang school of Chinese philosophy.

Romaji: (JPN) "Roman letters." Refers to Japanese words written with English letters.

Sha qi: (CHN) Energies directed at a site or running through a site that injure or overwhelm those who live or work there.

Sun Tzu: (CHN) "Master Sun." Military strategist and author of *The Art of War*, the most influential writing on the strategy of war in China.

Tai Ji Tu: (CHN) "The Supreme Ultimate." The symbol of yin and yang joined in dynamic union within the One.

Tianqi or **Tienchi:** (CHN) This refers to the energy of heaven meaning more directly, the energy of weather. Pronounced "*Otenki*" in Japanese.

Tokonoma: (JPN) An alcove near the entry of Japanese buildings and in important rooms in which calligraphy or painted scrolls, ikebana arrangements or art works are displayed prominently.

Traditional Chinese Medicine or **Jing-lo:** (CHN) The system of meridians and qi energy flow forms the basis for the five-thousand-year-old healing system of acupuncture and herbal medicine.

Wade-Giles: (CHN) An older, alternate system for writing Chinese word sounds with English letters. See *Pinyin*.

Wealth Corner: This refers to the corner of a room diagonally opposite the entry. It is a high focus area that is most magnetic both in drawing attention and in manifesting the symbols contained there.

Wu: (CHN) "Emptiness." Refers to the fundamental character of all created conditions and beings, including humankind, that have no independent existence, but arise only in connection with one another. *Mu* is the Japanese pronunciation of the character.

Xiansheng: (CHN) "Previous Birth," or "Previous Being." Title meaning Master of a particular Way, art or trade. It is reserved for great accomplishment. Although it is the same kanji as the Japanese "Sensei," the connotations are quite different.

Xin (CHN) or **Shin** (JPN): This means both heart and mind.

Yang: (CHN) "Banners waving in the sun." One of two penultimate powers emanating from the One (see *Tai Ji Tu*). Also means "district of light." Always paired and compared with yin.

Yin: (CHN) "Cloudy, obscure." One of the two penultimate powers emanating from the One (Tai Ji Tu). Also means "district of darkness." Always paired with yang.

Yinyuan: (CHN) This refers to the pre-existing affinity of two people, families or companies. It suggests a close connection and mutually beneficial relationship.

Zen: (JPN) Mahayana "Meditation" school of Buddhism transmitted from India to China, then to Japan in the 13th Century A.D. in the Rinzai, Soto and Obaku sects.

Zendo: (JPN) "The Way of Zen." Refers to the practice of meditation in the Zen tradition. Sometimes, it may refer to the hall in which Zen meditation is practiced.

INDEX

Altars, 59, 62, 67, 139, 140

Ba gua, 61, 163
   mirror, 61
Backyards, 128, 129
Bad neighbors, 131
Bankruptcy, xii, 47
Bars, 129
Bodhisattva, 131, 163
Buddhism, 25, 163, 168
Buyer/occupants, 40, 42

Client Relationships, 15
Confucianism, 25, 163
Confucius, 163
Contracts, 11, 16, 57, 93
Corner houses, 128

Dan Tian, 164
Dao, 34, 35, 164, 165
Dao de Jing, 164
Daoism, 25, 164
Dead Flora, 135
Death, 19, 28, 45, 46
Decision Influencers, 83
Divorce, 46

Estates, 28
EMF, 1, 133, 134

Feng shui
   cosmological feng shui, 36, 164
   cultural feng shui, 34, 36
   definition, 1, 2, 5, 13, 164
   energetic feng shui, 37
   feng shui dao, 35, 36, 164
   form feng shui, 36
   journal, 145, 146
   power feng shui, 35, 166
   symbol feng shui, 36
Fountains, 136
Fu dogs, 60, 61, 128

General Kwan, 60
Goals, 15, 16, 32, 33, 36, 38, 55, 62–65, 67–69, 80, 88, 151

Harmony, xiv, 13, 95, 148
Heart, 142, 143, 150, 168
Heirs, 28
History, 16, 33, 39, 41, 57
House numbers, 130

I Ching, 61, 87, 165
Ichi Go Ichi E, 72
Intuition, 143, 148

John Keats, 23
Jupiter, 97-99, 106, 155–162

Lao Tzu, 1, 165
Law of Correspondence, 87
Leaks, 6, 135
Luo Pan, 165

Master Quan, 63, 166
Mantra, 63, 166
Marriage, 43, 46
Mars, 61, 96, 97, 155–162
Meetings, 72, 73, 77, 79–83, 85, 105, 106
    Yang meetings, 74, 75
    Yin meetings, 75–77
Mercury, 91–93, 106, 155–162
Ming Shu, 166
Mirrors, 6, 61, 137
Moon, 65, 89–91, 106, 154

Negative capability, 23
Neptune, 102, 103, 155–162

Owner, xi, 8, 21, 39, 43, 47, 52, 122, 126
Occupant, 5, 8, 39, 42, 43, 45

Place, xiv, 1, 2, 5, 8, 52, 67, 71, 85, 87, 142, 149
Planetary Direction Changes, 155–162
Pluto, 104, 106, 155–162

Qi, 37, 166, 167

Retrograde, 91–94, 98, 102, 166
Rituals, 54, 56
    Celebration, 64, 65
    Centering, 59
    Clearing, 58
    Creation, 58
    Daily Water Aspiration, 66
    Emptying, 21, 55
    Protection, 60–62
    Purification, 29
    Seeding, 62–64
River Lo Map, 166

Saturn, 99–101, 106, 155–162
Sickness, 45
Solar and Lunar Eclipses, 90, 106, 152, 153
Staging, 109, 118
Station Point, 91

Taiji, 37, 167, 168
Tianqi, 2, 167
T-squares, 128

Uranus, 101, 102, 106, 155–162

Venus, 95, 96, 106, 155–162
Water, 2, 66, 130
Wealth Corner, 80–82, 118, 121–123, 127, 167
Webs of Relationships, 11–14
Wind, 1, 2, 35, 58, 131, 164
Wish fulfilling gem, 151
Wu, 167

Wu Xing, 165

Xin, 142, 143, 149, 168

Yang, 37, 73–75, 77–80, 87, 168

Yin, 37, 73–77, 79, 80, 87, 168

Yinyuan, 18, 19, 168

Zoning, 13, 14, 34

About the Authors

Anita J. Govert

Anita Govert began playing with feng shui in 1988 while working at California State University, Long Beach. Shortly after "feng shuing" her administrative office, she accepted a better position in Seattle.

Pursuing the study of feng shui with even greater interest, Anita combined her advancing studies and feng shui experience with a practice in residential real estate in 1998. She integrated feng shui perspectives with sustainability and green building practices leading her to serve as the VP of SustainableAZ.org, a non-profit promoting sustainability in building, landscaping and lifestyle.

Anita is an active Realtor® and Associate Broker at Tierra Antigua Realty, LLC in the Tucson area. She serves the Tucson real estate community as a member of the Tucson Board of Realtors Green Forum. She holds the designations the National Association of Realtors®, Green, the National Home Building Association Green™ Professional and is a certified Ecobroker®. Specializing as a buyers' agent in new home purchasing, Anita has worked with clients and contractors in exacting a balance among feng shui, sustainability, locality and budget concerns.

Johndennis P. Govert

Author of *Feng Shui: Art and Harmony of Place*, Johndennis Govert has practiced the art of feng shui as home owner, consultant, and teacher for over forty years. Traveling internationally, he has consulted with families, businesses, corporations and government and taught for colleges and professional realty, design and construction associations. Johndennis has an MBA in planning from Northwestern University and has been a licensed realty agent in Arizona for twelve years. His extensive business experience forms the core of Johndennis' feng shui practice. Johndennis also has extensive learning and discipline in the spiritual aspects of the art of feng shui. He is a practitioner of many of the Zen arts and is a transmitted Zen master in his own right. Johndennis has been a lifelong student and teacher of many of the ancient Asian wisdom traditions. In Seattle, Johndennis was a founder and first president of the Northwest Institute of Acupuncture and Oriental Medicine, a Traditional Chinese Medicine college, advancing professional education for skilled healers and providing wholistic health care options for the American public. Johndennis incorporates his knowledge and skill of healing into his practice and teaching of feng shui.

About REALty Feng Shui

REALty Feng Shui: Places and Profits in the Marketplace is a very practical guide about how to leverage real estate profits using the ancient Chinese design art of feng shui. From the color of the front door to meeting dynamics, *REALty Feng Shui* provides buyers and sellers of real estate and their realty agents with a way to improve the property, the process and profits simultaneously with greater win-win satisfaction. *REALty Feng Shui* de-mystifies the feng shui perspective and explains it in clear and modern terms and applies it in particular to the quick turnaround of the real estate market. It seems there are innumerable and inscrutable rules that constitute feng shui, but this book gives a simple and straightforward method for putting feng shui concerns into a contemporary perspective and applying them to enhance the experience of buying and selling real estate.

Ryo means understood, comprehended and also completed. In Zen shodo calligraphy, it usually serves as the seal of completion in realizing enlightenment. Here after a long, escrow ordeal it signifies successful completion of mutual benefit expressed with flair.

www.ingramcontent.com/pod-product-compliance
Lightning Source LLC
Chambersburg PA
CBHW080848020526
44118CB00037B/2315